**SQL LANGUAGE**

MW01293949

# FROM ZERO
# TO SQL IN
# 20 LESSONS

## CARLOS L CHACON

# LEGAL

# TABLE OF CONTENTS

# IS THIS BOOK FOR YOU?

This book was written for someone who is starting with zero or near zero information about the SQL language and wants to learn how to query a database. If you are a student or a professional looking to get more involved in analytics, reporting, or database development, this book is for you. While the concepts we explore can be applied to different databases, I concentrate on and all my examples are tested in Microsoft SQL Server.

The book can also be used as a reference for those who have started their training and need to refer back from time to time. Perhaps you need a bit of a refresher as it has been some time since your last query and you need to focus on a specific area. There is something here for you too. You can start with any chapter, get the specifics, and then be on your way—you don't have to read every chapter.

The goal is help you become more familiar with the SQL language and to help ensure you feel confident about the results of your queries.

If you think I missed something or should have done it better, let me know. Maybe you think I did a good job—I want to hear about that too. You can email me personally at carlos.chacon@sqldatapartners.com. I look forward to hearing from you.

## INDIVIDUAL SUPPORT

If you would like individual support or have questions about whether getting into analytics or databases is for you, the private Facebook page "Zero to SQL" has been created to help you do just that. With many community members ready to help you succeed, there has never been a better time to get help! For more information on how you can get personalized SQL help, visit our page http://zerotosql.com/facebook/ to get additional information about us and if the group is right for you.

## ABOUT THE AUTHOR

Carlos L Chacon is the owner of SQL Data Partners LLC, a consultancy providing database performance tuning for medical organizations with the GE Centricity application. He has over 10 years of experience working with databases and he holds a Bachelor's degree in Information Technology from Utah Valley State University. He currently resides in Richmond Virginia with his family, but enjoys traveling the world. He is also the co-host of the SQL Data Partners Podcast, which can be found on ITunes and Google Music or at his website http://sqldatapartners.com/podcast.

## TECHNICAL REVIEW

No one can write a program—or a book—without errors, and I am no different; however, thanks to my friends, those errors will be much harder to find. Should you find an error, let us know at http://zerotosql.com/feedback.

For helping me catch these errors, I will invite you to participate in our community page on Facebook.

Jamie Wick reviewed the technical details and made sure I stayed in line with standards. Jamie works for the College of William and Mary in Williamsburg VA as an engineer supporting Microsoft SQL Server. He is active in the local SQL community and is an avid photographer. You can catch him on twitter at @Jamie_Wick.

## LEAVING A REVIEW

If you have found the information in this book useful, I invite you to leave a positive review on Amazon.com.

 **CONVENTIONS USED IN THIS BOOK**

Represents a key point or something I want you to pay special attention to.

 Represents a new word or term that may be confusing.

 These draw attention to something you should do or not do. Some of this might be personal preference.

 Represents advanced topics or items to consider as you increase your learning.

# LESSON 1
# WHAT IS SQL?

*This lesson introduces some history on SQL and helps us understand why we do what we do.*

SQL has been described as a language where we tell the computer what we want and give it the information it needs to go and get it. Computers tend to be VERY literal, and you will need to give very specific instructions or you may be unhappy with the results. Bad data is a serious issue to deal with and we will want to make sure we are getting back the correct results from every query.

## ANSI STANDARD

Because there are several different database vendors, there are a set of standards that must exist across the database platforms. ISO (the International Organization for Standardization) is a worldwide federation of national standards bodies (ISO member bodies) and they came up with the set of standards that indicate how the SQL Language should be used. This standard allows us to use the same queries in each of the relational databases on the market. Each vendor, however, can come up with their own SQL statements for their databases to assist the data professional, but these SQL statements are considered proprietary and may need to be changed before the query can be run on a different vendor's database system. The standard that most database systems follow is called SQL-92. The 92 stands for 1992. Yikes! I wasn't even out of high school then and my kids tell me I am an old geezer now. There are now many differences between database vendors and their SQL implementations. This books seeks to introduce the basic features, which are part of the SQL-92 database standard.

## FIRST THINGS FIRST

Let's define a few concepts used throughout the book.

- **RDBMS** stands for Relational Database Management System. The RDMBS is your database—it could be Access, SQL Server, Oracle, or DB2 among others. The concepts presented here can be used in different systems; however, the examples have been verified in SQL Server.
- **Syntax** is the technical requirement the query must have to return the results you want. If the query is not properly formed, a result cannot be given. Think of proper sentence structure—should a question not end with a question mark? Syntax is similar to grammar rules. If you don't follow the rules your query won't work. Each query can have several components and each component may have a requirement. When we talk about Syntax we are referring to what the RDBMS needs to process your query.

## DATABASES SUPPORTED

The following examples should work in all the major RDMBS systems; however, I have chosen to focus on SQL Server. The scripts provided have been verified in SQL Server. Want to see another database supported? Please let me know at carlos.chacon@sqldata partners.com or you can help add to the scripts on GitHub at https://github.com/carloslchacon/ZeroToSql.

### RUNNING EXAMPLE

To help illustrate the SQL concepts in this book, I will use one of the first examples I was given when the light finally clicked in terms of certain SQL Syntax situations. This idea is only to help the learning process and I will note at the end of the book some of the shortcomings of this concept in 'the real world'. In this case, we will use a system for collecting information about pets with a few details about their owners. These are divided into two main groups—cats and dogs. We will build on our knowledge and include fish later in the book. I have also chosen to include some veterinarian information in this example.

The scripts to create a sample database and all the examples I use in this book are found at http://zerotosql. com/zerotosqlscripts. Appendix 1 at the end of the book describes how to use these scripts to get up and running.

## SQL EXAMPLES

All the data in the sample database was created by people working on this book. There is no 'real' data in the book; however, we did try to have a little fun and provide some examples you might be familiar with. The SQL examples show the syntax and the results of each query; however, in many cases the number of rows returned was simply too large to post in the book. Any modification to the results is noted and is done for formatting purposes.

Words that are *italicized* are table names, column names, or, in some cases, database terms. They are marked to show they are part of the examples.

Keywords are bolded when used in a sentence. If you have a color copy they will also be in color. Keywords also use the Consolas font (The font this paragraph is in.).

## SUMMARY

We use the SQL language to talk to our databases and each vendor has their own take on the language. This book focuses on the basics that can be used in most systems.

# LESSON 2
# DATABASE
# STRUCTURE

*This lesson reviews the pieces of a database and discuss how they fit together to help you form your queries.*

If you have ever been to a sandwich shop, you have seen a long counter with containers of various lengths and sizes. Each of these containers has a specific purpose— some hold meat, others hold cheese, and others hold vegetables; there are even containers for the sauces. However, as a customer you may not need or want each item from every container to be on your sandwich. All of a sudden I am feeling very hungry.

Your database is set up in a similar fashion. There are different buckets for different components of the system. We call these components objects and our challenge as a data professional is to use the appropriate objects, or ingredients if you are hungry, to satisfy the needs of our client—an end user or an application. This book focuses on two types of objects—tables and views—we will review how to create them and get data in and out.

## TABLES

A SQL table is a container for the database to hold your data. A kitchen table in my house might only hold a plate, a fork, and a cup. A table set for a fine French restaurant might hold several plates, a bowl, wine glasses, napkins, candles, and more silverware than you know what to do with. A table in a database can be the same way. Some will be very simple and others will have many components to it. You decide how you want to describe your data; each item you want to describe is a table. Let's talk about some of the basic structures of a table. I think it will be helpful to continue the comparison to the sandwich counter.

We mentioned that each container was a specific size and had a specific purpose. I shouldn't put meat in the lettuce container and the reverse is also true. In the case of a table, I have these containers and I need to put something specific in each one. Each container is represented by a column, and the specific type of data that goes inside the column is called a data type.

## COLUMNS AND DATA TYPES

The blessing and curse of the relational database system is you can describe in simple terms or in very complex terms the data in a table. There is a joke among database administrators that for all the features in relational database systems, the most popular database software in the world is Microsoft Excel. Part of this is because it is so easy to start categorizing and describing our data; however, in a real sense this is exactly how data is broken up in our relational database system. Each piece of information we want to track is put into a column and those columns have specific data requirements.

Our data requirements are called Data Types. They help describe the type of information we are looking to put in our column—text, a date, a number, a yes/no field. In fact, once we establish a data type, other types of data will not be allowed in that column.

## VIEWS

Views are queries we save for later use. They normally remove the complexity of the database from an end user so it makes it easier to get to the data. We can pull information from a view using a select statement; however, views don't contain data and are based on tables.

 Some RDMBS systems have indexed views that do contain data; however, that is beyond the scope of this book.

## ROWS

The item we are trying to collect data on, and all the information about the item, makes up our row. This is also sometimes called a record.

## PRIMARY KEYS

In our relational system we want a way to make each row unique so we can tell them apart and ensure when we query the table we will be able to identify each row. To assist us in this we use a primary key—a column or combination of columns that contain values that uniquely identify each row in the table. Most often this is a number that simply increments as a new row is added, but has no meaning to the data in the table. Sometimes a primary key can be used from the data we are collecting—we can identify a column that will not repeat.

Primary Keys become very important when we try to relate one table to another. We will get into this in lesson 6 on joins under Foreign Keys.

## SCHEMA

A schema is the owner of a database object. As we are just beginning, all the objects in the database will have only one owner; however, if you use third party applications you might see additional schema owners. A good practice example can be found in the AdventureWorks database provided by Microsoft. Schemas are helpful when we want to apply security to a database. We will touch more on this in the lesson on Security.

 Microsoft Access does not have a concept of Schemas.

## DATABASE DIAGRAMS

As you become more familiar with the syntax of writing queries, you will need to become more familiar with the structure of the data. One of the tools available to help visualize the database is a database diagram. Each RDBMS has their own way of providing you this information. I want to highlight only a few things here.

Image 1 is a Database Diagram of the model we will be working with at the beginning of the book. We will look at Cats, Dogs, and Owners. An owner can have one or more cats and could also have one or more dogs; perhaps they have none. Our database will attempt to collect some information about owners and their pets. With the exception of the Primary Key, I have chosen to keep the column names in alphabetical order to help assist in determining the similarity or differences of the tables; however, this order is not the way you might normally collect this information so I hope it does not cause confusion.

Image 1 Database Diagram

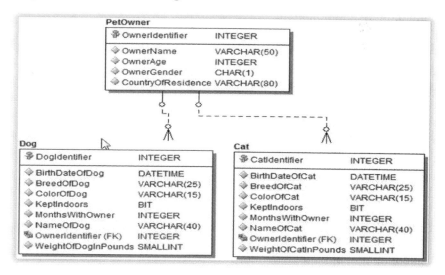

Image 1 illustrates the tables along with the column names and data types. The table names are outside the boxes and the PRIMARY KEY is on the first line with the key icon. The tables are related by the *OwnerIdentifier* column which we will discuss on our section on joins.

Image 2 Table Relationship

 Diagram 1 also uses some symbols to give additional information about how the tables connect. At the top of Image 2, we see a small circle with a single leg. This means there can be zero or one. At the bottom of Image 2, we see a small circle with three legs. This means there can be zero, one, or many. So, for example, in our table, a *PetOwner* can have zero, one, or many *Dog*. A *Dog* can have zero or one *PetOwner*. We will explore this further in Lesson 6 on Joins.

**SUMMARY**

Databases are made of various pieces like tables which have columns with data types. We normally think of a piece of data as a row. Tables in our database are related.

**HELP ME BUILD THE DATABASE**

If you would like to help me build the database structure for future books or examples by adding tables or data, you can join us at GitHub for the latest build at https://github.com/carloslchacon/ZeroToSql.

If you are so inclined, I look forward to working with you on this.

# LESSON 3
# RETRIEVING DATA

*This lesson looks at how we can retrieve data from our database.*

I once heard someone say that Microsoft Excel is the most popular database in the world. Thinking of our table as a spreadsheet can be helpful when first trying to retrieve data from the database. Using Image 3 as a guide, how would you identify what color and breed Jack is?

I would probably use the *Name* column and then look at the *Breed* column and then the *Color* column. The one advantage you have is you can skim with your eyes. Computers can't do that and we need a way to describe to the database what we are looking for.

Image 3 Spreadsheet on dogs

| Dog Id | Breed | Color | Name | Owner Id |
|---|---|---|---|---|
| 500 | Abruzzenhund | Yellow | Odie | 1 |
| 501 | Afador | Brown | Laddie | 3 |
| 502 | Bergamasco | Tan | Jack | 6 |
| 503 | Berger de Picard | White | Ace | 9 |
| 504 | Berger des Pyrenees | Gray | Ace | 12 |

Retrieving data from a database revolves around the SELECT statement. Remember, SQL describes what we want out of the database and this description starts with the word SELECT. Just as when we order a sandwich we select certain containers, with SQL, we SELECT the columns we want and then indicate which table those columns are in. We use the keyword FROM to specify the table name. Here is what the syntax looks like.

```
SELECT [column name]
FROM [table name]
```

We have the option of specifying each individual column or we can request all the columns in the table—much like a sandwich with 'everything'. If we wanted all the columns in our table, we can use the * operator and the columns will be displayed in the same order they are found in the table.

```
SELECT *
FROM Cat;
```

*While all RDBMS environments do not currently require a semicolon at the end of the statement, most have indicated they will require it in some future version. We will end all our statements with a semicolon.*

For formatting purposes, I only included the first 7 columns. Only the first 10 rows are displayed; however, your result will include more columns and rows.

Output
(Modified)

| Cat Identifier | BirthDate OfCat | BreedOfCat | ColorOfCat | Kept Indoors | Months WithOwner | NameOfCat |
|---|---|---|---|---|---|---|
| 1000 | 06/19/1978 | Tabby | Orange | 1 | 444 | Garfield |
| 1001 | 01/01/2008 | Abyssinian | Yellow | 1 | 12 | Ellie |
| 1002 | 11/15/2012 | Aegean | White | 1 | 13 | Dexter |
| 1003 | 01/21/2010 | American Curl | Brown | 1 | 14 | Elsa |
| 1004 | 02/16/2004 | American Bobtail | Orange | 1 | 15 | Loki |
| 1005 | 04/13/2003 | American Shorthair | Grey | 1 | 16 | Bella |
| 1006 | 04/13/2004 | American Wirehair | Grey | 1 | 17 | Lucy |
| 1007 | 05/16/2013 | Arabian Mau | Red | 1 | 18 | Luna |
| 1008 | 06/16/2012 | Australian Mist | White | 1 | 19 | Kitty |
| 1009 | 01/01/2013 | Asian | Black | 0 | 20 | Piper |

The SELECT * statement will give us every row and every column we have from the *Cats* table. We could also specify only certain columns to be returned, as shown in the queries below. When we specify the columns, we separate them with a comma.

```
SELECT NameOfCat,
BreedOfCat, ColorOfCat
FROM Cat;
```

```
SELECT NameOfDog,
BreedOfDog, ColorOfDog
FROM Dog;
```

OUTPUT
(Modified)

| NameOfCat | BreedOfCat | ColorOfCat | NameOfDog | BreedOfDog | ColorOfDog |
|---|---|---|---|---|---|
| Garfield | Tabby | Orange | Odie | Abruzzenhund | Yellow |
| Ellie | Abyssinian | Yellow | Laddie | Afador | Brown |
| Dexter | Aegean | White | Benji | Bergamasco | Tan |
| Elsa | Curl | Brown | Ace | Berger | White |
| Loki | Bobtail | Orange | Ace | Pyrenees | Gray |
| Bella | Shorthair | Grey | Benji | Bernese | Black |
| Lucy | Wirehair | Grey | Benji | Bernese | Black |
| Luna | Mau | Red | Benji | Bhagyari | White |
| Kitty | Mist | White | Benji | Berner Chow | Red |
| Piper | Asian | Black | Benji | Bernefie | Yellow |

The order in which we place the column names in the query determines the order we will see the columns in the results. We can put them in any order. You will notice in the second query the columns in the results are not in the same order the columns are listed in the table.

*SELECTING FROM TABLES OR VIEWS*

There is no difference to the RDBMS if we SELECT from a view or a table. All the examples here will work with views or tables.

## Special Select Options
We have a few operators available to help us limit the rows of data we want. We will discuss more advanced filtering options in Lesson 4.

# DISTINCT OPERATOR

There may be times when we want to see only one item in a list even though it may appear many times in the database. The keyword DISTINCT will return a single result for each unique value in the column. This example returns only one record for each of the dog colors we have in our table.

```
SELECT DISTINCT ColorOfDog
FROM Dog

OUTPUT
ColorOfDog
-----------------------------
Black
Black and White
Brown
```

```
Gray
Red
Tan
White
White and Yellow
Yellow
(9 row(s) affected)
```

If you add another column to the statement, the distinct will take the combination of the two columns. Let's add the column *BreedOfDog* to the statement.

```
SELECT DISTINCT ColorOfDog, BreedOfDog
FROM Dog
```

OUTPUT
(Modified)

```
ColorOfDog    BreedOfDog
----------    -------------------------
Black         Bernese Rottie

Black         Bleu de Gascogne
Black         Border Collie
Black         Broodle Griffon
Black         Bukovina Sheepdog
Black         Bulldog
Black         Cairland Terrier
Black         Cambodian Razorback Dog
Black         Care-Tzu
Black         Carolina Dog
```

(176 row(s) affected)

In the case of the column *ColorOfDog*, you will get duplicates rows; however, the combination of color and breed will only appear once.

## TOP OPERATOR

We may want to have only a certain number of records returned. The keyword TOP will allow us to limit the number of rows returned. You can either set the number of rows to return or you can set a percentage. The keyword PERCENT is used to indicate a percentage of the rows needed.

```
SELECT TOP 5 OwnerName, OwnerAge, OwnerGender
FROM PetOwner
```

```
OUTPUT
OwnerName                OwnerAge    OwnerGender
---------------------    ----------  -----------
Jon Arbuckle             40          M
James Jones              50          M
Sophia                   60          F
John Smith               25          M
Emma Davis               70          F
(5 row(s) affected)
```

```
SELECT TOP 1 PERCENT OwnerName, OwnerAge, OwnerGender
FROM PetOwner
```

```
OUTPUT
OwnerName                OwnerAge    OwnerGender
---------------------    ----------  -----------
Jon Arbuckle             40          M
James Jones              50          M
Sophia                   60          F
John Smith               25          M
(4 row(s) affected)
```

## SUMMARY

When we want to retrieve data from a table, we use the SELECT statement. We can retrieve all columns using the * symbol or retrieve only certain columns by specifying a name. We can also limit the number of records by using the keywords DISTINCT or TOP.

# LESSON 4
# FILTERING

*This lesson reviews the way we can limit or qualify the records that are returned.*

In most cases, we will not want every single row in the table and we need a way to identify which rows we want returned. We can add a filter to the query and limit the rows returned. While performance tuning is beyond the scope of this book, you would be surprised at the number of issues I have encountered because of bad filtering or no filtering at all. If you see a query that has no filter—be wary.

We can filter on most types of information available in our table. Examples include date criteria, a quantity criteria, or a specific last name. The main objective is to make sure we are asking the right question. Once we know what we are looking for, we can apply our filter with the keyword WHERE. We then choose our filter column and apply the type of filter we want. Some types of filters include: *Equal To* ( = ), *Less Than* ( < ), and *Greater Than* ( > ). Other filters are in Table 1 below. Check the index if you are looking for something specific.

In this example, we will look for cats with the name of Garfield. We will use the *Equal To* operator on the column *NameOfCat* to find this information.

```
SELECT NameOfCat, BreedOfCat, ColorOfCat
FROM Cat
WHERE NameOfCat = 'Garfield';
```

```
OUTPUT
NameOfCat               BreedOfCat              ColorOfCat
----------------        ------------------      ----------------
Garfield                Tabby                   Orange
```

You will notice there are quotes around the word Garfield in our statement. This is because the column *NameOfCat* is a text field and we want to indicate to the database server what kind of data we are working with. The single quotes help with this.

If we wanted to find all of the dogs who have been with their owners for less than 2 months, we could use the *Less Than* operator ( < ) on the *MonthsWithOwner* column as shown in the query below.

Table 1 List of Operators

| Operator | Operator Symbol |
|---|---|
| Less than | < |
| Greater than | > |
| Not equal to | <> (Less than and greater than) |
| Equal to | = |
| Less than or equal to | =< OR <= |
| Greater than or equal to | >= OR => |

```
SELECT NameOfDog, BreedOfDog, ColorOfDog
FROM Dogs
WHERE MonthsWithOwner < 2;
```

The results here have not been modified. We will only get back 9 records from this query.

```
OUTPUT
NameOfDog              BreedOfDog              ColorOfDog
-------------------    --------------------    ------------
--------
Odie                   Border-Aussie           Gray
Rover                  Cairnoodle              Tan
Rover                  Cairoston               White
Spike                  Cane Corso Italiano     Tan
Spike                  Cherokee Monarch        Yellow
Clifford               Chow Pei                Yellow
Dief                   Dachshund               White and
Yellow
Doc                    Dakotah Shepherd        Yellow
Rover                  La Pom                  Tan
(9 row(s) affected)
```

## Special Filter Operators

There are several operators we can use to assist us in filtering. They include LIKE, IN, and NOT IN. There are few others, but these are the most common.

### Like

Let's say we're looking for a cat, but couldn't quite remember its name; however, we know it started with Gar. We can use the LIKE operator to help us find the list of names that start with Gar. We should only use the LIKE operator with text data types.

There are two components to using the LIKE operator. The first is using the actual word LIKE in the WHERE clause. The second is the use of the wildcard character % inside our character string. The % symbol tells the database we will accept anything that matches the text we have entered. In this case, the query would look like this

```
SELECT  NameOfCat, BreedOfCat
FROM    Cat
WHERE   NameOfCat LIKE 'Gar%';
```

```
OUTPUT
NameOfCat          BreedOfCat
----------------   ------------------------------
Garfield           Tabby
Gareth             Snowshoe
Gary               Sokoke
Garth              Somali
Garret             Turkish Angora
Garth              Russian Tabby
Gary               American Curl
Gareth             American Shorthair
Garret             Brazilian Shorthair
(9 row(s) affected)
```

In this query, we could get back Cat names like Garfield, Gary, Garth, Gareth, Garret, and Gargamel. With the keyword LIKE, we use part of a phrase to compare against the possible values in the database. Where there is a match, those rows get returned to us.

An advanced use of the wildcard operator would be to search for the middle of a word. For example, if we changed our query to WHERE NameOfCat LIKE 'Gar%h' (notice the h at the end), we would only get names like Garth and Gareth because in this example they start with Gar, but end with h.

IN

We may want to find records that match a list or a set number of possibilities. We may want to only find dogs with the names Pluto, Lassie, Benji, and Old Yeller. The keyword IN will allow us to provide a list of names to search. We separate each search criteria (in this case, name) with a comma. In this example we are using the string data type in the *NameOfDog* column. To use the list, I enclose the names with parentheses, and use single quotes before and after each name.

```
SELECT   NameOfDog , BreedOfDog , ColorOfDog
FROM     Dog
WHERE    NameOfDog IN ( 'Pluto', 'Lassie', 'Benji', 'Old
         Yeller' );
```

```
OUTPUT
NameOfDog         BreedOfDog             ColorOfDog
--------------    ----------------------  ---------------
--------
Pluto             Bloodhound             Yellow Orange
Benji             Tibetan Terrier        Black
Old Yeller        Chacy Ranior           White
Benji             Chihuahua              Yellow
Lassie            Border Collie          Light Brown and
White
(5 row(s) affected)
```

Let's say we only wanted to see owners with an even age between 8 and 16 years old. I don't know why we might want this, but sometimes it is fun to poke at the data a bit. This time *OwnerAge* is a numeric column so we don't need to add the single quotes, but we do need to separate each number with a comma.

```
SELECT OwnerName, OwnerAge, OwnerGender
FROM PetOwner
WHERE OwnerAge IN (8,10,12,14,16);
```

```
OUTPUT
OwnerName                    OwnerAge    OwnerGender
------------------------     ----------  -----------
```

| | | |
|---|---|---|
| Ava | 14 | F |
| Christoper | 12 | M |
| Steven | 14 | M |
| Layla | 10 | F |
| Terry | 10 | M |
| Gerald | 12 | M |
| Keith Urbon | 14 | M |
| Samuel Lamanite | 16 | M |
| Ralph Rice | 10 | M |
| Lawrence Arabia | 12 | M |
| Nicholas Cage | 14 | M |
| Roy Orbison | 16 | M |
| Hailey | 14 | F |
| Gary | 16 | M |
| Clarence Angel | 14 | M |
| Sean | 16 | M |

(16 row(s) affected)

## NOT IN

We may want to exclude certain items from our result set. We may want to exclude the names Old Yeller and Odie. The keyword NOT IN will allow us to provide a list to exclude from the search. We separate each exclusion criteria (in this case, name) with a comma. In this example we are using the string data type in the *NameOfDog* column. We will enclose the name with parentheses, and use single quotes before and after each name.

```
SELECT NameOfDog, BreedOfDog, ColorOfDog
FROM Dogs
WHERE NameOfDog NOT IN ( 'Hercules',
'Spike','Pongo','Ace','Clifford','Laddie','Rover');
```

OUTPUT
(Modified)

| NameOfDog | BreedOfDog | ColorOfDog |
|---|---|---|
| Odie | Abruzzenhund | Yellow |

```
Jack            Bergamasco              Tan
Jack            Bernese Mountain Dog    Black and
White
Jack            Bernese Rottie          Black
Jack            Bhagyari Kutta          White and
Yellow
Pluto           Bloodhound              Yellow Orange
Dingo           Carolina Dog            Gray
Diogenes        Carolina Dog            Black and
White
Einstein        Bleu de Gascogne        Black
Flash           Bloodhound              White and
Yellow
(122 row(s) affected)
```

## Combining Operators

We can include as many conditions to our query as we want. We can set multiple conditions on the same column or we can use two or more columns to help decide what should be returned. Two conditions could be given and if either of them contain a match, the corresponding rows will be returned.

When we have two or more conditions and we want every condition to be met, we use the keyword AND. When we have two or more conditions and we want any one of the conditions to be met, we use the keyword OR.

Let's say we wanted to limit our search to the names of a few dogs, and we also wanted only those dogs who have been with their owners for at least 2 years. This is really the combination of the two examples in the IN clause section. We will use the keyword AND because we want both conditions to be met.

```
SELECT NameOfDog, BreedOfDog, ColorOfDog
FROM Dogs
WHERE NameOfDog IN ('Pluto', 'Lassie', 'Benji', 'Old
       Yeller')
       AND MonthsWithOwner > 24;
```

```
OUTPUT
NameOfDog              BreedOfDog              ColorOfDog
----------------       ------------------      ----------------
Pluto                  Bloodhound              Yellow Orange
Benji                  Tibetan Terrier         Black
(2 row(s) affected)
```

Adding the keyword AND between the two conditions tells the database they both have to be met for a row to be returned.

If we switched this up a bit and used the keyword OR, then our results would include dogs whose names are in the list OR who have been with their owners for at least 2 years, even if their names are not in the name list.

```
SELECT NameOfDog, BreedOfDog, ColorOfDog
FROM   Dogs
WHERE  NameOfDog IN ('Pluto', 'Lassie', 'Benji', 'Old
       Yeller')
       OR MonthsWithOwner > 24;
```

```
OUTPUT
(Modified)
NameOfDog              BreedOfDog              ColorOfDog
----------------       ------------------      ----------------
Odie                   Abruzzenhund            Yellow
Pluto                  Bloodhound              Yellow Orange
Hercules               Carolina Dog            Black and White
Hercules               Carolina Dog            Black
Hercules               Carolina Dog            White and Yellow
Clifford               Carolina Dog            Red
Clifford               Bulldog                 Yellow
```

```
Clifford          Carolina Dog      Brown
Clifford          Carolina Dog      Tan
Clifford          Carolina Dog      White
(116 row(s) affected)
```

 We will occasionally make our queries a little too specific and no data may result. If we are sure we are asking the right question, no data returned is ok.

## SUMMARY

We can limit or filter the records that get returned from our queries. Our statements will often include a WHERE clause, and there is no limit to the number of options we can include in the WHERE clause.

# LESSON 5
# SORTING DATA

*This lesson discusses how we can sort or order our data for presentation.*

As we present the results of a query to those who will use the data, we will often want to sort the information to help us make sense of it. We can normally sort by any of the columns in our table. There are two ways to sort data: Ascending (A-Z, 1-10) and Descending (Z-A, 10-1). We use another keyword in SQL to indicate this: ORDER BY. By default, all of our statements will use the Ascending order keyword ASC to sort the data. If we want the data sorted Descending, we need to use the keyword DESC.

Using the example of all the cats that start with GAR, using the keyword LIKE, and sorting by the name of the cat, our query would look like this:

```
SELECT NameOfCat, BreedOfCat, ColorOfCat
FROM Cats
WHERE NameOfCat LIKE 'Gar%'
ORDER BY NameOfCat;
```

```
OUTPUT
NameOfCat            BreedOfCat             ColorOfCat
---------------      ---------------------  --------------

Gareth               Snowshoe               White
Gareth               American  Shorthair    Grey
Garfield             Tabby                  Orange
```

```
Garret            Brazilian Shorthair    Brown
Garret            Turkish Angora         Grey
Garth             Russian Tabby          Grey
Garth             Somali                 Brown
Gary              Sokoke                 Grey
Gary              American Curl          Grey
(9 row(s) affected)
```

This puts the results of the query in alphabetical order by the name of the cat so it will be much easier to find the cat we are looking for. In the query below, I added the ASC keyword to the query; however, to the database it is the same as the query above.

```
SELECT NameOfCat, BreedOfCat, ColorOfCat
FROM Cats
WHERE NameOfCat LIKE 'Gar%'
ORDER BY NameOfCat ASC;
```

```
OUTPUT
NameOfCat            BreedOfCat              ColorOfCat
---------------     ----------------------  --------------
Gareth              Snowshoe                White
Gareth              American Shorthair      Grey
Garfield            Tabby                   Orange
Garret              Brazilian Shorthair     Brown
Garret              Turkish Angora          Grey
Garth               Russian Tabby           Grey
Garth               Somali                  Brown
Gary                Sokoke                  Grey
Gary                American Curl           Grey

(9 row(s) affected)
```

If we wanted the cats listed in reverse alphabetical order, our query would look like this:

```
SELECT NameOfCat, BreedOfCat, ColorOfCat
FROM Cats
WHERE NameOfCat LIKE 'Gar%'
ORDER BY NameOfCat DESC;
```

OUTPUT

| NameOfCat | BreedOfCat | ColorOfCat |
| --- | --- | --- |
| Gary | Sokoke | Grey |
| Gary | American Curl | Grey |
| Garth | Russian Tabby | Grey |
| Garth | Somali | Brown |
| Garret | Turkish Angora | Grey |
| Garret | Brazilian Shorthair | Brown |
| Garfield | Tabby | Orange |
| Gareth | Snowshoe | White |
| Gareth | American Shorthair | Grey |

(9 row(s) affected)

In the above query, we find we have three cats with the name Garfield. We also see the breed order is not in alphabetical order. SQL gives us the option to sort or ORDER BY more than one column. This is useful when the first column has duplicate data and we need a second criteria to use for sorting. Again, ASC is assumed by the database.

```
SELECT NameOfCat, BreedOfCat, ColorOfCat
FROM Cats
WHERE NameOfCat LIKE 'Gar%'
ORDER BY NameOfCat, BreedOfCat;
```

OUTPUT

| NameOfCat | BreedOfCat | ColorOfCat |
| --- | --- | --- |
| Gareth | American Shorthair | Grey |
| Gareth | Snowshoe | White |
| Garfield | Tabby | Orange |
| Garret | Brazilian Shorthair | Brown |
| Garret | Turkish Angora | Grey |
| Garth | Russian Tabby | Grey |
| Garth | Somali | Brown |

```
Gary              American Curl         Grey
Gary              Sokoke                Grey
```

(9 row(s) affected)

We can also sort column in different directions. If we wanted to sort our list by the length of time a cat has been with their owner, and then by the name of the cat, our query would look like this:

```
SELECT NameOfCat, BreedOfCat, MonthsWithOwner
FROM Cats
WHERE NameOfCat LIKE 'Gar%'
ORDER BY MonthsWithOwner DESC, NameOfCat ASC;
```

```
OUTPUT
NameOfCat       BreedOfCat            MonthsWithOwner

--------------  --------------------  ---------------
Garfield        Tabby                 444
Garth           Somali                165
Gary            Sokoke                162
Gareth          Snowshoe              161
Gary            American Curl         87
Gareth          American Shorthair    70
Garth           Russian Tabby         65
Garret          Turkish Angora        49
Garret          Brazilian Shorthair   5
```

(9 row(s) affected)

The cats with longer time with their owners will be displayed first, and each cat with the same *MonthsWithOwner* will be listed in alphabetical order. What's more, we are sorting by a column we have not asked for in the result set. What will be returned is *NameOfCat*, *BreedOfCat*, and *ColorOfCat*. *MonthsWithOwner* will not be displayed in the result. We can use ANY of the columns in our table to manipulate our results.

We don't, in fact, even have to order by the name of the column, we can simply state the column number. Be careful with this one—your code will undoubtedly change, and you could inadvertently change the order of your result set because you failed to update the ORDER BY columns. For this reason, I strongly recommend against this approach.

```
SELECT NameOfCat, BreedOfCat, MonthsWithOwner
FROM Cats
WHERE NameOfCat LIKE 'Gar%'
ORDER BY 1, 2;
```

OUTPUT

| NameOfCat | BreedOfCat | MonthsWithOwner |
| --- | --- | --- |
| Gareth | American Shorthair | 70 |
| Gareth | Snowshoe | 161 |
| Garfield | Tabby | 444 |
| Garret | Brazilian Shorthair | 5 |
| Garret | Turkish Angora | 49 |
| Garth | Russian Tabby | 65 |
| Garth | Somali | 165 |
| Gary | American Curl | 87 |
| Gary | Sokoke | 162 |

(9 row(s) affected)

## SUMMARY

The ORDER BY keyword allows us to sort our data in different ways. We can sort columns in different orders and we can also sort by virtually every column in our table.

# LESSON 6
# JOINS

*The way we connect tables or views to get a broader result is discussed in this lesson.*

Dearly Beloved, we are gathered here today . . . the classic opening line for marriage ceremonies. Okay, so the marriage analogy doesn't work so well, but bringing data together is like a marriage—you are going to join two objects together and if the relationship is going to work they need to have something in common.

Until this point, we have only queried a single table. If we were to look at this visually, our tables exist separately, and we have interacted with only one at a time.

## Image 4 SELECT FROM a single TABLE

**SELECT FROM TABLE**

Each table returns every row for the columns selected

```
SELECT NameOfDog,
BreedOfDog
FROM Dog

SELECT NameOfCat,
BreedOfCat
FROM Cat
```

## FOREIGN KEYS

RDBMS includes the word relational, indicating that the objects in our database should relate to one another. When we want to relate tables, at least one column of the same information should be included in the tables we want to relate. The primary reason I chose the Cat, Dog, and owner example is because it helps to illustrate the relationship in a clear way. A *PetOwner* can have a dog, but a dog may not necessarily have an owner. When a dog does have an owner, there is a hierarchy—the owner owns the dog. We can use this hierarchy to then establish a relationship. When a dog has an owner, the owner can then be used to help describe the dog.

In our database, an owner can have zero dogs, one dog, or many dogs. We are using the OwnerIdentifier column to identify an owner in our database. When we add the OwnerIdentifier column to the Dog table—to help describe the dog--we can create a foreign key in the Dog table. A foreign key is a column or combination of columns that is used to establish and enforce a link between the data in two tables. This allows us to create a relationship between our tables. This relationship is shown by the line between the two tables. This relationship helps the RDBMS know about the relationship.

## Image 5 Foreign Key Relationship

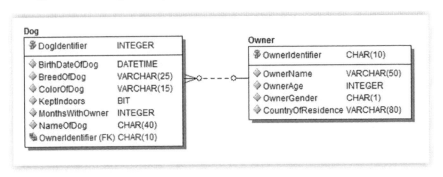

Each of these tables has a column named *OwnerIdentifier* and a foreign key has been created on the Dog table. Both columns are the same data type. While you can join on columns of different data types, the best practice is to make the column data types the same.

 While two tables have columns with the same name, this does not create the foreign key relationship. A foreign key must be created when the relating table (in this case, Dog) is created or can be created afterwards. If the database diagram does not show the relationship with a line, the foreign key has not been created.

Now that we know the columns that each table shares in common, we can join them; however, the type of join we use will depend on the question we are trying to ask. For example, do we want to find only people with cats that don't have a dog? Do we want to find only people that have a dog and no cats? Do we want to find people that have at least one cat and one dog? Answering this question will then tell us which type of join to use.

## INNER JOIN

An INNER JOIN is used to get rows that match in each table. In this instance we want to know which cats also live with a dog—each pet must have the other. If they don't, they won't show up in our results. When they have to exist in both tables, we use an INNER JOIN.

To help us understand this relationship, it may be helpful to visualize the relationship. In this case we are going to join the Dog table and the Cat table. When an owner has both a cat and a dog, the pets will appear in our query.

Image 6 Inner Join

**INNER JOIN**

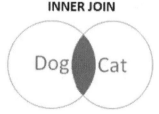

Each table returns rows for only those who own Dogs AND Cats

```
SELECT NameOfCat,
NameOfDog
FROM Cat
INNER JOIN Dog ON
Cat.OwnerIdentifier =
Dog.OwnerIdentifier
```

The syntax for a join query is to specify the join type and then the table to be joined. We then use the keyword ON with the relationship columns. Our INNER JOIN example will look like this:

```
SELECT [NameOfCat], [NameOfDog]
FROM Dog
INNER JOIN Cat ON Dog.OwnerIdentifier =
Cat.OwnerIdentifier;
```

```
OUTPUT
(Modified)
DogIdentifier  NameOfDog  BreedOfDog                    NameOfCat
-------------  ---------  ----------------------------  ----------
500            Odie       Beagle                        Garfield
743            Aragorn    German Shorthaired Pointer    Arwen
579            Spike      Border Collie                 Bella
586            Jake       Border Collie                 Bella
747            Murry      Jack Russell Terrier          Bella
749            Rover      Labrador Retriever            Lucy
751            Pongo      Lancashire Heeler             Luna
753            Rex        Maltese                       Kitty
582            Spike      Border Collie                 Piper
589            Lila       Braque du Bourbonnais         Piper
755            Rover      Large Munsterlander           Piper
```

Here we can see the cat Bella has 3 dogs in her home. Because she matches on more than one record in the dog table, she is listed for matched record in the dog table.

The database will join on anything.

If we really wanted to, we would also see which dogs and cats have the same names. It doesn't mean they have the same owners, but the database will let us join the tables together on just about any column we choose—although, it is possible to get an error in some cases. Sometimes this can lead to bad data. Foreign keys help us know which columns we should join.

## LEFT OUTER JOIN

We use a LEFT OUTER JOIN when we want to see all the rows of one table and any rows that match our join criteria from the second. Each join syntax is similar, so you won't be surprised to see the keyword LEFT OUTER JOIN is used to define the join along with the keyword ON and the join criteria. In this query all rows from the table listed first (the left) will be returned, and only the matching rows from the second table (right table) will be included.

```
SELECT DogIdentifier, NameOfDog , BreedOfDog , NameOfCat
FROM Dog
LEFT OUTER JOIN Cat ON Dog.OwnerIdentifier =
Cat.OwnerIdentifier;
```

```
OUTPUT
(Modified)
DogIdentifier NameOfDog BreedOfDog          NameOfCat
------------- --------- ------------------- ---------------
500           Odie      Abruzzenhund          Garfield
501           Laddie    Afador                NULL
502           Jack      Bergamasco            NULL
503           Ace       Berger de Picard      NULL
504           Ace       Berger des Pyrenees   Jake
504           Ace       Berger des Pyrenees   Bella
505           Jack      Bernese Mountain Dog  NULL
506           Jack      Bernese Rottie        NULL
507           Jack      Bhagyari Kutta        NULL
508           Pluto     Bloodhound            Maggie
  (369 row(s) affected)
```

Here we are introduced to something called a NULL value—it is the database telling you it has no value for the data you query. In this case, there are several dogs who do not have cats in the home, so the *NameOfCat* column shows a NULL because there is no matching row.

> *You can also filter on whether a record has a NULL or NOT NULL value. When you want to ensure a value has data, you can use the keyword IS NOT NULL and the database will filter out any rows that don't have a value.*

Again, let's visualize what it is we are trying to query. In our example, we would see ALL the dogs in our database, and we will see each cat that is in the home with a dog.

Image 7 LEFT OUTER JOIN

For rows with dog names that have no cats in the same home, we will see a NULL value. A NULL Value means there is no data present.

**RIGHT OUTER JOIN**

We use a RIGHT OUTER JOIN when we want to get all the values from the table on the right, or the 'joined' table, and then see the matching data from the first table, or the table on the left. The now familiar join syntax will be RIGHT OUTER JOIN followed by ON with the join criteria. In order to help demonstrate this more clearly, I will order by the column CatIdentifier. I do this because I expect to see a record for every cat even if they don't have an accompanying dog record.

```
SELECT NameOfCat, NameOfDog, BreedOfDog
FROM Dog
RIGHT OUTER JOIN Cat ON Dog.OwnerIdentifier =
Cat.OwnerIdentifier
ORDER BY Cat.CatIdentifier;
```

```
OUTPUT
NameOfCat        NameOfDog        BreedOfDog
-----------      ---------------  ----------------------
Garfield         Odie             Abruzzenhund
Ellie            NULL             NULL
Dexter           NULL             NULL
Arwen            Aragorn          Labany
Milo             NULL             NULL
Bella            Murry            Labradoodle
Bella            Spike            Border Collie
Bella            Jake             Border Collie
Lucy             Rover            Labrador Retriever
Luna             Pongo            Lancashire Heeler
  (317 row(s) affected)
```

Remember—NULL values mean there is no information for that column.

Our visualization for a RIGHT OUTER JOIN would look like this.

## Image 8 RIGHT OUTER JOIN

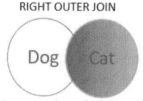

RIGHT OUTER JOIN

Returns each row from Cat and all matching Dog rows

```
SELECT NameOfDog,
BreedOfDog, NameOfCat
FROM Dog
RIGHT OUTER JOIN Cat
ON Cat.OwnerIdentifier
= Dog.OwnerIdentifier
```

Now you may be wondering here—What if I switched the order of the tables, could I use a Left Outer Join? Yes, you could. If you noticed that, go eat a piece of candy as your reward. ☺

Personal Preference: I rarely use RIGHT OUTER JOINs because it makes more sense to line up my columns 'from the left' and move right. For this reason, I use LEFT OUTER JOINs 99.99% of the time.

## SUMMARY

We have reviewed how you can join tables together to get additional information for our queries. While there are some additional join types, INNER JOIN and LEFT OUTER JOIN will cover you 99% of the time.

# LESSON 7
# MANIPULATING
# DATA AND ALIASES

*This lesson discusses how we can modify our data before we present it to the end user. To describe our modification, we use an alias.*

While the majority of cases will directly show the data we SELECT from a table, occasionally we will want to manipulate this data before we present it. Now, I am not suggesting a life of crime in 'cooking the books' or any such notion. I am suggesting a much more simple idea of modifying data so it is more presentable to the end user. Changing Date formats to a European standard would be an example; or making a calculation for the total of an invoice so the end user does not have to make this calculation. In some cases the data is not provided and we can make calculations to provide this data. For example, we might not have to know how old a person is, but if we have a birthdate, we can make a calculation to get how old the person is.

Our Cat table includes a column *MonthsWithOwner*. What if we wanted to present this information in years instead of months, we can make a simple math calculation by dividing the months by 12. I am also going to require a cat has been with an owner at least one year.

```
SELECT NameOfCat, MonthsWithOwner / 12 AS 'Years WITH
Owner'
FROM Cat
WHERE MonthsWithOwner > 12;
```

```
OUTPUT
(Modified)
NameOfCat        Years WITH Owner
--------------   ----------------
Garfield         37
Dexter           2
Arwen            2
Milo             3
Bella            4
Lucy             1
Luna             1
Kitty            1
Piper            1
  (147 row(s) affected)
```

Of course, we can make all the basic math calculations—addition, subtraction, multiplication, and division—on our numeric data types.

While some databases will allow you to make mathematical calculations on text fields, this should be avoided. While your testing may have worked, you have no idea what kind of data you will get in the future. This is a good example of why data types are important in a relational database.

## ALIASES

Because I made a calculation, best practice dictates I give the column a descriptive name using the keyword AS, and then the name surrounded by single quotes, because I have a space in the column name. Using the keyword AS with a name is known as aliasing. Giving an Alias is not required and the database will run the query without the AS 'Column Name' syntax; however, the column will have no name and this can get a bit tricky—or even not allowed as you write more sophisticated queries.

We can alias columns, tables, and views; however, don't make this your best trick. Reading aliases can be tricky, so remember—someone is eventually going to have to review your code. Make good alias names, because that reviewer just might be you. ☺

I also suggest you do not use keywords or reserved words as aliases. Any of the keywords we have mentioned should be avoided. Examples include group, order, count, max, etc.

When there are no spaces in the alias name, you are not required to use single quotes with the alias.

## CONCATENATION

When we want to combine columns of text data types, we concatenate the string or link a series of values into a single string. Databases use different syntax for this concatenation and we will review both types.

We want to create a single sentence out of some of the data we have—let's try something like 'Odie is a Yellow dog and he lives with Jon Arbuckle.' We have the NameOfDog, ColorOfDog and OwnerName in our database. What we don't have are the fragments 'is a' and 'dog who lives with', so we will have to add them to our query. We can't forget the punctuation either—this will give us a total of 6 components in our SELECT clause.

In SQL Server and MS Access, we will use the + sign to indicate concatenation and in other RDBMS we will use the || sign. Let's try it out.

```
SELECT NameOfDog + ' is a ' + ColorOfDog + ' dog who lives with
' + OwnerName + '.'
FROM Dog
INNER JOIN PetOwner ON PetOwner.OwnerIdentifier =
Dog.OwnerIdentifier
WHERE Dog.DogIdentifier < 510;


SELECT NameOfDog || ' is a ' || ColorOfDog || ' dog who lives
with ' || OwnerName || '.'
FROM Dog
INNER JOIN PetOwner ON PetOwner.OwnerIdentifier =
Dog.OwnerIdentifier
WHERE Dog.DogIdentifier < 510;
```

OUTPUT
SQLSentence
-----------------------------------------------------------
```
Odie     is a Yellow dog who lives with Jon Arbuckle.
Laddie   is a Brown dog who lives with Sophia.
Jack     is a Tan dog who lives with Robert.
Ace      is a White dog who lives with Ava.
Ace      is a Gray dog who lives with David Leal.
Jack     is a Black and White dog who lives with Zoe.
Jack     is a Black dog who lives with Joseph Abramson.
Jack     is a White and Yellow dog who lives with Madelyn.
Pluto    is a Yellow Orange dog who lives with Mickey Mouse.
Hercules is a Yellow dog who lives with Charlotte.
(10 row(s) affected)
```

You will notice each of the text components we added start and end in a single quote. Every time we want to add another part to the string, we use the + or || signs to denote we are continuing our string. Also notice there are no commas between the column names. This indicates we want all of the information to be returned in a single column. We can also add other columns to the final result of the query. Let's say we wanted to see each column we used above plus the full sentence. Our query would look like this.

```
SELECT NameOfDog, ColorOfDog, OwnerName,
NameOfDog + ' is a ' + ColorOfDog + ' dog who lives with
' + OwnerName + '.'
FROM Dog
INNER JOIN PetOwner ON PetOwner.OwnerIdentifier =
Dog.OwnerIdentifier
WHERE Dog.DogIdentifier < 510;
```

OUTPUT
(Modified)

| NameOfDog | ColorOfDog | OwnerName | SQLSentence |
| --------- | ---------- | --------- | ----------- |
| Odie | Yellow | Jon Arbuckle | Odie is a Yellow dog who lives with Jon Arbuckle. |
| Laddie | Brown | Sophia | Laddie is a Brown dog who lives with Sophia. |
| Jack | Tan | Robert | Jack is a Tan dog who lives with Robert. |
| Ace | White | Ava | Ace is a White dog who lives with Ava. |
| Ace | Gray | David Leal | Ace is a Gray dog who lives with David Leal. |
| Jack | Black and White | Zoe | Jack is a Black and White dog who lives with Zoe. |
| Jack | Black | Joseph Abramson | Jack is a Black dog who lives with Joseph Abramson. |
| Jack | White and Yellow | Madelyn | Jack is a White and Yellow dog who lives with Madelyn. |
| Pluto | Yellow Orange | Mickey Mouse | Pluto is a Yellow Orange dog who lives with Mickey Mouse. |
| Hercules | Yellow | Charlotte | Hercules is a Yellow dog who lives with Charlotte. |

(10 row(s) affected)

*WHY IS THERE WHITE SPACE BETWEEN THE NAME OF THE DOG AND THE REST OF THE SENTENCE?*

Great Question! The white space exists because the column *NameOfDog* in the dog table has a data type of CHAR(40). This means the column will be 40 characters wide. If a record does not contain forty characters, like Odie, the rest of the record will be filled with white space.

We will discuss data types in Lesson 17 and we will go into more detail about different data types.

## SUMMARY
We can manipulate columns in our statements so they can be better presented. Aliases are used to name columns when we do data manipulation. Data types can affect how our columns respond to manipulation.

# LESSON 8
# FUNCTIONS

*This lesson reviews calling already created logic so we don't have to reinvent the wheel.*

All of the aspects we have discussed in this book can be used in a variety of database systems and this is intentional. You may recall from the ANSI standard section that most databases support the standard that was created in 1992; and in technology standards, that is ages ago! I graduated from both high school and college and had five kids in that time! Functions are a clear example of how each vendor has decided to implement certain logic and to a degree is a differentiator between the database platforms.

*In Microsoft Access there are two types of functions—those you can use for VBA code and those for SQL Queries. We will only deal with those you can use for SQL queries in this book.*

## WHAT IS A FUNCTION?

A function is a little piece of code the database has to help you, the query writer, do routine tasks so you don't have to write the code each time. There are various types of functions, but they all behave in a certain pattern. While some functions are used outside of a table, it is best to think of a function in terms of a column and what you want to do with the data in the column.

## USING A FUNCTION

Each database will have snippets of code we can access by using the name of the function, and then passing the required information—normally just a single column name—inside of open and closed parentheses. Let's say for instance that we want to choose a name for our new dog and the database has a function we can use called ChooseNewName ( ).

## PARAMETERS

Because our database holds several pet options for us to choose from, we need to specify the type of animal we want to choose a name for. The type of pet we choose will become a parameter—a piece of information the function needs to complete the task. We input (or 'pass') the parameter to the function in the parentheses () next to the function name. We will pass a parameter value of `'Dog'` and our *ChooseNewName* function will return a name out of all the names in our *DogOwner* table. Our query would be as follows:

```
SELECT   ChooseNewName('Dog') AS NameOfDog;

OUTPUT
NameOfDog
-------------------
Rover
(1 row(s) affected)
```

In certain cases, a function can return a single row, or it could return a row for each qualifying row in the table. Part of using the function is understanding how it will affect our query. This is especially important when we start using our own home-grown functions.

A simple function we can try is to count all the rows in the table. Sure, we could simply select all the rows and see the result, but the database has a function we can use called COUNT. The * specifies that all rows should be counted to return the total number of rows in a table.

```
SELECT   COUNT(*) AS 'Total Number of Cats'
FROM     Cat;

OUTPUT
Total Number of Cats
-------------------
266
(1 row(s) affected)
```

A single row will be returned and the result will be the number of rows in our cat table.

 Do I always have to use a parameter? The answer depends on the function. Some functions may not return a value unless a parameter is given. A simple test—running the function without a parameter to see if you get an error—will let you know if you need to provide a parameter or not.

```
SELECT ChooseNewName ();
```

OUTPUT
An insufficient number of arguments were supplied for the procedure or function ChooseNewName.

## BASIC MATH FUNCTIONS

We can use some of the simple math functions—Min, Max, AVG, and SUM—as basic examples of functions we can use in our queries. Each uses the same format and you will notice we only have one column in our select query. I have also used an alias in each example query below.

## MIN

We use the MIN () function to determine the smallest amount or number in a column. While there may be more than one row with the smallest number, only one row will be returned.

```
Select MIN (MonthsWithOwner) AS LeastTimeWithOwner
FROM Cat;
```

OUTPUT
LeastTimeWithOwner
------------------
1

(1 row(s) affected)

# MAX

We use the MAX () function to determine the largest amount or number in a column. While there may be more than one row with the largest number, only one row will be returned.

```
Select MAX (MonthsWithOwner) AS MostTimeWithOwner
FROM Cat;

OUTPUT
MostTimeWithOwner
-----------------
444

(1 row(s) affected)
```

# AVG

We use the AVG () function to determine the average of all the values in a column. These examples use the columns MonthsWithOwner and OwnerAge

```
Select AVG (MonthsWithOwner) AS AvgTimeWithOwner
FROM Cat;

OUTPUT
AvgTimeWithOwner
----------------
37

(1 row(s) affected)

SELECT AVG(OwnerAge) AS 'Average Pet Owner Age'
FROM PetOwner;
```

```
OUTPUT
Average Pet Owner Age
---------------------
41

(1 row(s) affected)
```

As with the other functions, we can add a where clause to include only specific criteria. This example will give us the average pet ownership time for cats that are Orange.

```
Select AVG (MonthsWithOwner) AS AvgTimeWithOwner
FROM Cat
WHERE ColorOfCat = 'Orange';
```

```
OUTPUT
AvgTimeWithOwner
----------------
44
(1 row(s) affected)
```

## SUM

We use the SUM () function to determine the total value of all the rows in a column. This example uses MonthsWithOwner.

```
Select SUM (MonthsWithOwner) AS 'Total Months of Cat
Ownership'
FROM Cat;
```

```
OUTPUT
MonthsWithOwner
------------------
10055

(1 row(s) affected)
```

```
Select SUM (MonthsWithOwner) AS 'Total Months of Cat
Ownership for Black Cats'
FROM Cat
WHERE ColorOfCat = 'Black';
```

```
OUTPUT
MonthsWithOwner
------------------
1591
```

(1 row(s) affected)

## Advanced Numeric Functions

I must admit I have not frequently used the advanced number functions, but thought they deserved to be included. They are as follows:

Table 2 Other Function Types

| Function | How to call the function |
|---|---|
| Absolute Value | ABS () |
| Cosine | COS () |
| Exponential value | EXP () |
| The value of PI | PI () |
| Sine | SIN() |
| Square Root | SQRT() |
| Tangent | TAN () |

## SUMMARY

Functions let us packaged code for reuse at a later time. We can build our own functions, but in the beginning we can use many of the built-in functions to help us with our statements.

# LESSON 9
# SUMMARIZING
# DATA

*This lesson discusses how to group our data together so we can get totals and counts of our data.*

Now that we have gone over functions, we can look at summarizing or grouping the data together. While we have some functions that will look at the aggregate or whole of the data, what if we wanted to break it up a bit? For example, perhaps we are interested in finding the most common cat name in our system.

The idea of grouping is to identify how we are going to create our groups. In our cat name example, we may want to group or categorize the data by the column *NameOfCat*. We will add the keyword GROUP BY to our query and specify the name of the column we are grouping—*NameOfCat*. In my Select section, I will request two columns—the column I am grouping on and the function I need to count the number of names. I will also include the keyword ORDER BY so the data makes more sense. As I want to get the most popular cat name, I will order by the most popular first.

```
Select NameOfCat, COUNT(*) AS 'Number of Cats'
FROM Cat
GROUP BY NameOfCat
ORDER BY COUNT(*) DESC;
```

```
OUTPUT   (Modified)
NameOfCat              Number of Cats
-----------------      --------------
Bella                  7
Luna                   7
Olive                  6
Jax                    6
Milo                   5
Max                    4
Mittens                4
Molly                  4
Leo                    4
Lily                   4
(111 row(s) affected)
```

The result is a list of cat names with the number of times they appear in the database. The names are listed in order of most popular to least popular.

In our database, it appears Bella and Luna are tied for first with 7 cats with that name.

Ultimately, the question we must ask ourselves is what do we want to get out of the data? We can use another of the functions we introduced earlier to find the number of pet owners by country in our database. With the goal of making the data more readable, we want to order by the count in descending order for easy lookup of the most records.

```
SELECT CountryOfResidence, COUNT(*) AS NumberOfOwners
FROM PetOwner
GROUP BY CountryOfResidence
ORDER BY COUNT(*) DESC;
```

OUTPUT   (Modified)

| CountryOfResidence | NumberOfOwners |
| --- | --- |
| United States Of America | 57 |
| Great Britain | 48 |
| Costa Rica | 33 |
| Singapore | 31 |
| Tanzania | 23 |
| Argentina | 21 |
| New Zealand | 20 |
| Peru | 18 |
| Luxembourg | 18 |
| Kenya | 16 |

(27 row(s) affected)

Of course, we can group by more than one column—in fact, many times we will want to do this. Let's take our name example a bit further and include the gender of the owner in the statement. Since Country is the component I want to see first, I list CountryOfResidence first in the GROUP BY section, followed by Gender.

```
SELECT CountryOfResidence, OwnerGender, COUNT(*) AS
NumberOfOwners
FROM PetOwner
GROUP BY CountryOfResidence, OwnerGender
ORDER BY COUNT(*) DESC;
```

```
OUTPUT
(Modified)
CountryOfResidence              OwnerGender   NumberOfOwners
-------------------------------  -----------  ----------
----
United States of America        M                 36
Great Britain                   F                 25
Great Britain                   M                 23
United States Of America        F                 21
Costa Rica                      F                 21
Singapore                       F                 18
Tanzania                        F                 16
Argentina                       F                 13
Singapore                       M                 13
Luxembourg                      M                 13
  (44 row(s) affected)
```

A second twist I am putting on this query is I want to see the countries listed in alphabetical order, followed by the owner genders and then the number of owners. My ORDER BY clause has been updated to reflect this change. While the ASC is optional, I have included it to illustrate the logic of the query.

```
SELECT CountryOfResidence, OwnerGender, COUNT(*) AS
NumberOfOwners
FROM PetOwner
GROUP BY CountryOfResidence, OwnerGender
ORDER BY CountryOfResidence ASC, COUNT(*) DESC;
```

```
OUTPUT
(Modified)
CountryOfResidence              OwnerGender   NumberOfOwners
-------------------------------  -----------  ---------
Argentina                       F                 13
Argentina                       M                 8
Costa Rica                      F                 21
Costa Rica                      M                 12
Denmark                         F                 2
```

```
Djibouti                        F              1
Djibouti                        M              1
Dominica                        F              2
Dominican Republic              F              1
Dominican Republic              M              1
  (44 row(s) affected)
```

## FILTERING GROUPS

Just as we use the WHERE clause to limit the records returned, we can limit the groups returned, if they don't meet a specific criteria, using the keyword HAVING. HAVING will not remove rows from being eligible in our result; however, it will remove groups that don't meet the criteria we set.

As we continue to build on the number of owners from around the world, let's say we are only interested in seeing countries that have more than 10 pet owners.

```
SELECT CountryOfResidence, COUNT(*) AS NumberOfOwners
FROM PetOwner
GROUP BY CountryOfResidence
HAVING COUNT(*) > 10
ORDER BY COUNT(*) DESC;
```

```
OUTPUT
CountryOfResidence                NumberOfOwners
------------------------------    --------------
United States Of America          57
Great Britain                     48
Costa Rica                        33
Singapore                         31
Tanzania                          23
Argentina                         21
New Zealand                       20
Peru                              18
Luxembourg                        18
Kenya                             16
```

```
Israel                          14
Jamaica                         12
El Salvador                     12
```

```
(13 row(s) affected)
```

In this instance, the list will reduce by about half as we don't have enough records from many of the countries that qualify with at least 10 owners. The HAVING COUNT(*) > 10 component of our query will ensure there is no record in the *NumberOfOwners* column that is less than 10.

Just a reminder that if we wanted to include countries with exactly 10 owners we would have to use the >= comparison.

We can also join tables together and still use grouping. For example, if we wanted to get the most popular dog names by country, our query would look like this. I use the HAVING clause to eliminate some results for display purposes.

```
SELECT NameOfDog, PetOwner.CountryOfResidence, COUNT(*)
AS NumberOfOwners
FROM PetOwner
INNER JOIN Dog ON Dog.OwnerIdentifier =
PetOwner.OwnerIdentifier
GROUP BY NameOfDog, PetOwner.CountryOfResidence
HAVING COUNT(*) > 3
ORDER BY COUNT(*) Desc;
```

```
OUTPUT
NameOfDog      CountryOfResidence         NumberOfOwners
----------     ----------------------     --------------
Hercules       United States Of America        8
Pongo          United States of America        5
Spike          United States Of America        5
Spike          New Zealand                     5
Spike          Peru                            4
Clifford       Singapore                       4
```

```
Ace            Great Britain                      4
Butch          Great Britain                      4
Hercules       Great Britain                      4
Hercules       Luxembourg                         4
```

(10 row(s) affected)

I want to make another point of mentioning how the filter process works. A WHERE clause will either exclude rows or specify which row can be included. A HAVING clause will look at groups and then make a filter on the group. In our last example, Spike had the highest name count for the New Zealand. If we were to exclude New Zealand and the name of Spike, our results would be much different. I again use the having clause to limit the number of records returned.

```
SELECT NameOfDog, PetOwner.CountryOfResidence, COUNT(*)
FROM PetOwner
INNER JOIN Dog ON Dog.OwnerIdentifier =
PetOwner.OwnerIdentifier
WHERE CountryOfResidence <> 'New Zealand' AND NameOfDog
<> 'Spike'
GROUP BY NameOfDog, PetOwner.CountryOfResidence
HAVING COUNT(*) > 3
ORDER BY COUNT(*) Desc;
```

```
OUTPUT
NameOfDog      CountryOfResidence        NumberOfOwners
----------     ------------------        --------------
Hercules       United States Of America       8
Pongo          United States of America       5
Spike          United States Of America       5
Spike          New Zealand                    5
Spike          Peru                           4
Clifford       Singapore                      4
Hercules       Luxembourg                     4
```

(7 row(s) affected)

**SUMMARY**

We can use the keyword GROUP BY to put our data into groups—like going back to elementary school multiplication, only this time the database does the counting for us.

# LESSON 10
# SUBQUERIES

*This lesson deals with situations where you have to ask multiple questions of the data to get a result. You layer those questions in a subquery.*

Much like working with a group, sometimes there are multiple questions we want to ask of a group or a subset of data. To do this, we can create a query and then literally wrap another query around it to get additional details about this information. To help us understand how we might use a subquery, let's take a look at our Data Model and then ask a few questions. For space reasons, the tables in our diagram include only the table name and the primary key.

Image 9 Data model with veterinarian visit

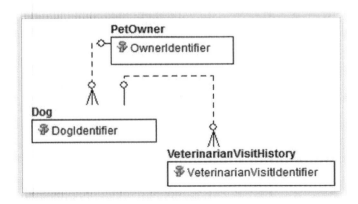

We see that an owner can have a pet—in this case, we are only showing dog. We can also see a pet can have a veterinarian visit. What if we wanted to see the owners who have dogs whose rabies shots are not current? Pet Owner doesn't link directly to the VeterinarianVisitHistory table. To do this query, we would first have find the dogs whose shot was not current. I am using a bit column to do this, which we review in Chapter 17. In this example a setting of zero means no and a 1 means yes.

```
SELECT DogIdentifier
FROM VeterinarianVisitHistory
WHERE RabiesShotCurrent = 0;
```

OUTPUT

```
DogIdentifier
-------------
551
541
551

(3 row(s) affected)
```

Now that we have the DogIdentifier for the owner, we can go to the Petowner table and query for the names of the pet owners.

```
SELECT OwnerName
FROM PetOwner
INNER JOIN Dog ON Dog.OwnerIdentifier =
PetOwner.OwnerIdentifier
WHERE Dog.DogIdentifier IN (541,551) ;
```

OUTPUT
OwnerName

--------------------------
Pipper Longstocking
Mike Smith
(2 row(s) affected)

Using a subquery will allow us to get this information in a single statement. The query format is not completely new and it does use several of the aspects we have discussed. A little formatting will help us to understand more clearly. We must alias the join query so we can complete our join criteria.

```
SELECT [ColumnName]
FROM [TableName]
JOIN (Select [ColumnName]
FROM [TableName]) [QueryAlias] ON [Join Criteria]
```

Our example would look like this. We use the alias of 'shot' to describe the query about which dogs do not have their shots current. We can use the dog identifiers to join to the dog table.

```
SELECT   PetOwner.OwnerName
FROM     PetOwner
         INNER JOIN Dog ON Dog.OwnerIdentifier =
PetOwner.OwnerIdentifier
         INNER JOIN ( SELECT VeterinarianVisitHistory.DogIdentifier
                      FROM   VeterinarianVisitHistory
                      WHERE  RabiesShotCurrent = 0
                    ) shot ON shot.DogIdentifier = Dog.DogIdentifier;
```

OUTPUT
OwnerName

--------------------------
Pipper Longstocking
Mike Smith
(2 row(s) affected)

This outline is only to help us understand the idea of a subquery. Now let's suppose we need to get a count of the owners and the number of times they have visited the veterinarian. Our query will have two columns in the results. You will notice we do a group by in our inner query and get a count (VetVisits). We can then use that count in the outer query and provide the VetVisit number to the final select.

```
SELECT OwnerName,
    visits.VetVisits AS 'Number of Vet Visits'
FROM  PetOwner
    INNER JOIN Dog ON Dog.OwnerIdentifier = PetOwner.OwnerIdentifier
    INNER JOIN ( SELECT DogIdentifier ,
                    COUNT(*) AS VetVisits
               FROM   VeterinarianVisitHistory
               GROUP BY VeterinarianVisitHistory.DogIdentifier
               HAVING COUNT(*) > 1
             ) visits ON visits.DogIdentifier = Dog.DogIdentifier;
```

The output looks like this.

```
OwnerName                      Number of Vet Visits
--------------------------     --------------------
Sean Conary                    2
Scott Tissue                   2
(2 row(s) affected)
```

The exciting part of subqueries comes when we start using our aggregate functions and can combine them with other data to show the users the end result.

## Summary

A subquery is a query that is nested inside a SELECT, INSERT, UPDATE, or DELETE statement, or inside another subquery. This gives us a logical format to break a query into pieces. The subquery will return a result that the remaining query can then process.

# LESSON 11
# INSERTING DATA

*This lesson discusses how to add records
to your tables.*

To this point, we have focused on getting data out of our database systems; however, we will eventually want to add data to the tables in our database. This section will review the syntax of how to insert data.

## COLUMN REQUIREMENTS

We have discussed the name and the data type of a column. A part of the table we have not yet discussed are the requirements of each column. Certain columns of the table are required—like a primary key; however, not every column must have data. Think of a form you recently filled out—did you leave part of it blank? We can specify which of our columns are required to have data and which are not required. This knowledge about the column will become important as we construct our insert statements.

Table 3 Condition Requirements

| Condition | Explanation |
|---|---|
| NOT NULL | The column must be present in an insert statement |
| NULL | The column is not required for an insert statement |

In our *Cat* table, let's take a second look at the table, but this time include the requirement conditions in the third column.

Image 10 Database Diagram with requirements

| Cat | | |
|---|---|---|
| CatIdentifier | INTEGER | IDENTITY |
| BirthDateOfCat | DATETIME | NULL |
| BreedOfCat | VARCHAR(25) | NULL |
| ColorOfCat | VARCHAR(15) | NOT NULL |
| KeptIndoors | BIT | NOT NULL |
| MonthsWithOwner | INTEGER | NULL |
| NameOfCat | VARCHAR(40) | NOT NULL |
| OwnerIdentifier (FK) | INTEGER | NULL |

We can insert all the columns in the table in a single insert statement; however, the column is not required unless the column in the table has a NOT NULL condition. In our Cat table, the values we must insert include:

CatIdentifier – This is automatically done for us by the system. This was done when we created the table and we discuss this further in lesson 13 in the creating tables section.

ColorOfCat – this has a VARCHAR (variable length) data type.

KeptIndoors – This has a Bit (yes/no) data type.

NameOfCat – This column has a VARCHAR data type.

Just as the saying goes—"The more, the merrier" —we should look to include as much information as we can in our insert statement. But occasionally we might look to provide the absolute minimum, though we shouldn't make it a habit.

The syntax to build an insert statement which includes ALL the columns looks like this--

INSERT INTO [TableName] [ColumnNames] VALUES [ListOfValues]

Our Cat table would look like the statement below. In this instance we are inserting all the columns except for the primary key, which the database will assign for us. You will notice the data we want to insert must be in the same order as the columns we specify.

```
INSERT INTO [Cat]

([BirthDateOfCat],[BreedOfCat],[ColorOfCat],[KeptIndoors]
,[MonthsWithOwner],[NameOfCat],[OwnerIdentifier])
    VALUES ('01/01/2014', 'Himalayan', 'Gray', 0, 18,
'Shadow', 84);

OUTPUT
(1 row(s) affected)
```

In this example, we are inserting all the columns, so we aren't required to provide the column names. This statement and the above statement are the same.

```
INSERT INTO [Cat]
        VALUES ('01/01/2014', 'Himalayan', 'Gray', 0, 18,
'Shadow', 84);
OUTPUT
(1 row(s) affected)
```

## CREATING INCOMPLETE ROWS

When we do not want to insert all of the columns, we must specify the columns we are inserting. This is especially true if we are using an auto-incremented number, like our primary key. This example shows the insert for only the required columns.

```
INSERT INTO [Cat]
        ([ColorOfCat],[KeptIndoors],[NameOfCat])
    VALUES
        ('White', 0, 'Dru');
OUTPUT
(1 row(s) affected)
```

This example will create a cat record; however, we won't have an owner and we won't know what breed of cat we have. We will come back to this record when we talk about changing data in lesson 12.

## INSERTING DATA FROM ANOTHER TABLE

We can insert data by specifying each value as we do with an insert statement; however, we can also copy or move data that already exists in a table to another table. We can combine our knowledge of an insert statement with a select statement to copy data. We could even copy just a subset or even a query where we do some calculation of data into another table.

Our syntax for inserting data by selecting data from another table looks like this:

```
INSERT INTO [TableName] ([NameOfColumn],[NameOfColumn])
 SELECT [NameOfColumn],[NameOfColumn])
 FROM [TableWithData]
```

We have a table name AnimalsToBePlaced that has both cats and dog in the table. We want to put this information into the appropriate table. This is a common scenario when data might be loaded into a temporary or staging table, and then we have to move the data to the appropriate data. Often we do some data manipulation before we insert the data. In this example, we only need to insert the data into the appropriate table. We will use the WHERE clause to accomplish this.

```
INSERT INTO Dog
( BirthDateOfDog ,BreedOfDog ,ColorOfDog ,KeptIndoors ,
MonthsWithOwner ,NameOfDog ,OwnerIdentifier)
SELECT BirthDateOfAnimal ,BreedOfAnimal ,ColorOfAnimal
,KeptIndoors ,MonthsWithOwner ,NameOfAnimal
,OwnerIdentifier
FROM AnimalsToBePlaced
WHERE TypeOfAnimal = 'Dog';

OUTPUT
(7 row(s) affected)


INSERT INTO Cat
( BirthDateOfCat ,BreedOfCat ,ColorOfCat,KeptIndoors ,
MonthsWithOwner ,NameOfCat ,OwnerIdentifier          )
SELECT BirthDateOfAnimal ,BreedOfAnimal ,ColorOfAnimal
,KeptIndoors ,MonthsWithOwner ,NameOfAnimal
,OwnerIdentifier
FROM AnimalsToBePlaced
WHERE TypeOfAnimal = 'Cat';
OUTPUT
(7 row(s) affected)
```

We will insert 7 records into both the dog and cat tables.

**Creating Tables on the Fly**
In the example above, the tables were already created for us and we simply populated them. We can also create a table 'on the fly,' or at runtime of the query, and the database will use the data returned to create the column names and data types. This should really only be used in testing or for temporary reporting needs. Primary Keys do not get created in this; however, data types get copied over and some RDBS implementations will copy the NULL requirement setting. We will go over how to create tables later in lesson 13.

In this scenario our syntax changes a bit. We begin with the select syntax and then use the keyword INTO and the name of the table we want to create. When we complete this query a new table will be created for us.

```
SELECT [NameOfColumn],[NameOfColumn])
INTO [NewTableName]
FROM [TableWithData]
```

In our example we will create a new table called DogsInEstablishedHomes. If you try to query from this nonexistent table now, you will receive an error.

```
SELECT * FROM DogsInEstablishedHomes;

OUTPUT
Invalid object name 'DogsInEstablishedHomes'.
```

Now, let's look at the query we will use to create this new table.

```
Select NameOfDog, BreedOfDog, ColorOfDog, MonthsWithOwner
INTO DogsInEstablishedHomes
FROM Dog
WHERE MonthsWithOwner > 24;
```

OUTPUT
(116 row(s) affected)

Once the query has been run and the table created, a query to pull data from the table will execute successfully and the results will be returned.

```
SELECT * FROM DogsInEstablishedHomes;
```

OUTPUT
(Modified)

| NameOfDog | BreedOfDog | ColorOfDog | MonthsWithOwner |
|-----------|------------|------------|-----------------|
| Odie | Abruzzenhund | Yellow | 442 |
| Pluto | Bloodhound | Yellow Orange | 300 |
| Hercules | Carolina Dog | Black and White | 25 |
| Hercules | Carolina Dog | Black | 26 |
| Hercules | Carolina Dog | White and Yellow | 27 |
| Clifford | Carolina Dog | Red | 28 |
| Clifford | Bulldog | Yellow | 29 |
| Clifford | Carolina Dog | Brown | 30 |
| Clifford | Carolina Dog | Tan | 50 |
| Clifford | Carolina Dog | White | 49 |

(116 row(s) affected)

## SUMMARY
We not only can query data out of tables, but we now have some ways to add data to our tables.

# LESSON 12
# MAKING CHANGES
# TO DATA

*This lesson discusses modifying our data
when changes occur.*

In addition to querying and inserting data, we will need to change some data from time to time. The most important component of any data change is the WHERE clause. Why is this so important? If you fail to include a where clause the change will affect EVERY row in the table!! Many a horror story can be told about failing to put a WHERE clause before a change and then having to recover data as a result.

We will get into the syntax, but remember the WHERE clause—you have been warned. ☺

## UPDATES

As the name implies, when we want to make a change to the data, we will use the keyword UPDATE. We then indicate what table we are going to update. The keyword SET indicates which columns we want to change. The most important component is our WHERE clause which puts limits on the rows that will be updated.

```
UPDATE Cat
SET NameOfCat = 'Mr. Whiskers'
WHERE NameOfCat = 'Whiskers';
```

```
OUTPUT
(4 row(s) affected)
```

This changes the *NameOfCat* of 'Whiskers' to 'Mr. Whiskers'. Don't forget to put single quotes around all the text options.

We can continue to build on what we have learned and do more complex statements. Here we are going to update the MonthsWithOwner column of the cat table because we found an error with owners from Russia. We only want to update those records, so we can use the INNER JOIN syntax and put a WHERE clause to update only the records we want.

```
UPDATE Cat
SET MonthsWithOwner = MonthsWithOwner + 2
FROM Cat
INNER JOIN PetOwner ON PetOwner.OwnerIdentifier =
Cat.OwnerIdentifier
WHERE PetOwner.CountryOfResidence = 'Russia';
```

```
OUTPUT
(2 row(s) affected)
```

## DELETE

We will want to remove data—occasionally—maybe. Our databases are getting bigger and bigger because we are keeping more data. In fact, many times I normally move old data to another table instead of deleting it; however, we do run across data we do want to delete. We use the keyword DELETE followed by the table we are deleting from. We will generally (99% of the time) include a WHERE clause, unless you want to remove ALL the data from the table. You have been warned—don't forget the WHERE clause. In this example, 2 test records have been created we can delete.

```
DELETE
FROM Dog
WHERE Dog.NameOfDog = 'Test';

OUTPUT
(2 row(s) affected)
```

 Many applications use a flag to indicate if a record has been deleted. There may be a column called IsDeleted where 0 means the record is usable and 1 means the record should not be used by the application. In virtually all of the SELECT statements, we would need to add a WHERE IsDeleted = 0 to get the rows we care about. Another option to remove data is to archive the data to another table. We did mention how to move data from one table to another; however, the process of archiving data is beyond the scope of this book.

## SUMMARY
We can modify the data through the use of the UPDATE and DELETE keywords

# LESSON 13
# CREATING OBJECTS

*This lesson discusses how we can create
tables to help us build our database.*

Now that we have reviewed how to get data in and out of our database, chances are you will want to create some objects to help support your database and/or your application. We will take a look at how to create tables, views, and stored procedures.

## CREATE TABLES

As we have discussed, our tables are made up of columns and each column needs a data type. We should also indicate whether the column is required, and designate one of our columns as a primary key.

```
CREATE [TableName]
(
 ColumnOneName DataType (size) {Requirement}
 , ColumnTwoName DataType (size) {Requirement}
)
```

*PERSONAL STYLE* - I put the comma on the second line because that is how I like to style my code. The create statement could be on one line—we separate the various lines for readability.

CREATE [TableName] ( ColumnOneName DataType(size) {Requirement}, ColumnTwoName DataType(size) {Requirement})

To the database, these two example statements are the same. Formatting makes the code easier to read for us humans.

Let's imagine we decide to start collecting information in our database on pet owners who have fish as pets. We want to create a new table to capture this information. Our CREATE TABLE statement will look like this:

```
CREATE TABLE Fish
    (
      FishIdentifier INT
    , BirthDateOfFish DATETIME NULL
    , BreedOfFish VARCHAR(30) NULL
    , ColorOfFish VARCHAR(25) NOT NULL
    , MonthsWithOwner INT NULL
    , NameOfFish CHAR(40) NOT NULL
    , OwnerIdentifier INT NULL
    , TankSizeInGallons SMALLINT NULL
    , PRIMARY KEY NONCLUSTERED ( FishIdentifier )
    ) ;


OUTPUT
Command(s) completed successfully.
```

Executing this statement will create the table, add all of the columns to the table, and make the *FishIdentifier* column the Primary Key. It will not; however, create an auto sequence number for the primary key and we don't go into any detail about that option in this book; however, more detail can be found at http://zerotosql.com/AutoIncrement. The scripts provided with this book include the creation of the auto increment for the Primary Key. We discussed foreign keys in lesson 6 and the fact that we need to create the Foreign Key. For example, although *VeterinarianVisitHistory* has a column called *FishIdentifier*, the Foreign Key has not yet been created. In the database diagram below, notice there is no line between *Fish* and *VeterinarianVisitHistory*. This indicates to us a Foreign Key has not yet been created.

Image 11 New Table With No Foreign Key Relationship

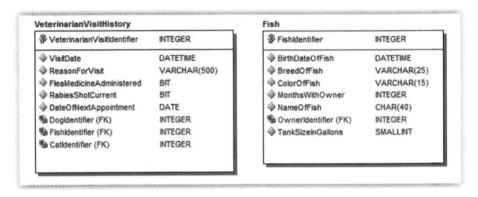

## CREATING A FOREIGN KEY

To create the relationship between two tables, we need to create a foreign key. This is created using the alter command, so we will review this in Chapter 16.

### Column Requirement

Many database systems do not require you to specify whether the column is required when you create or modify a table. If this is not specified the default is NULL, meaning no value is required. While you might be tempted to make this a habit—you will be surprised how many queries you won't be able to make because you don't have enough data. Sometimes requiring information is a good database decision.

Primary Keys columns automatically default to required; however, Foreign Keys have the option of allowing a NULL option. In our database, this would allow us to insert a new row into the dog table without requiring an owner, and this makes sense. On the other hand, having a record in the *VeterinarianVisitHistory* without an animal doesn't make any sense, so a requirement to have an animal makes sense when creating that record.

### Creating other types of objects

We can also create views, triggers, functions, stored procedures, users and roles. Views are discussed in greater detail in the next lesson. The other objects are considered more advanced topics and are not addressed in this book.

## Auto Incrementing Primary Key

Because each RDBMS implements this a little differently, I have not included this component in the book. For information on how your RDBMS implements auto incrementing columns, please visit http://zerotosql.com/autoincrement. The code needed to create the incrementing primary key for the fish table is included with the scripts in the download section at http://zerotosql.com/zerotosqlscripts.

## SUMMARY

We can create tables and specify the columns and datatypes we need to store our data.

# LESSON 14
# VIEWS

*This lesson discusses views—their purpose and function.*

We use Views to remove complexity for an end user by saving a query for future use. Writing a statement where the select is from a table or from a view looks identical, so database architects will often begin the name of a view with a prefix v_ or vw. This is not required, but helps assist a developer or a Database Administrator to know what type of object they are working with.

The syntax for creating a view uses the keywords CREATE VIEW and then we name the view and use the keyword AS. We encapsulate our query with open and closed parentheses.

```
CREATE VIEW [ViewName]
AS
(
 SELECT FROM TABLE
)
```

We can create a view for our database to store the logic needed to find all the cats named Garfield.

```
CREATE VIEW v_SearchForGarfield
AS
(
Select *
FROM Cat
WHERE Cat.NameOfCat = 'Garfield'
);
OUTPUT
Command(s) completed successfully.
```

After we create this view, we can now use it in a select statement to retrieve the results we are looking for. Notice we no longer need the where logic to get the results we are looking for—they are already included in the view.

```
SELECT * FROM v_SearchForGarfield;
```

```
OUTPUT
NameOfCat                    ColorOfCat
------------------------     --------------
Garfield                     Orange

(1 row(s) affected)
```

 All versions of RDBMS systems allow for security in the database. This allows us to control who sees what objects. Depending on your RDBMS, others may not be able to see the objects you create until you give them permission.

While we can use views to hide the complexity of a query, don't make a habit of creating views from views. This process, called nesting, can make queries very difficult to troubleshoot and can lead to performance problems.

## SUMMARY

Views are like saved queries to help us make data easier to access.

# LESSON 15
# SECURITY

*This lesson discusses some of the security considerations for your database and how you can implement them.*

Security is often an afterthought in most databases and I will not suggest creating Fort Knox in this volume; however, a brief overview of security is in order. After all, thinking about who will be accessing your data might play a role in how you create it. We will discuss the concept of roles, schemas, and how you can allow people to see or use only part of the database.

You can give an individual user permission to objects in your data and avoid roles altogether; however, this is not efficient and will lead to increased effort in applying security. Using Roles and Schemas allow you to decrease the administrative effort in applying security.

## ROLES

"Many hands make light work" is a phrase I really like and believe to be true. When just one person does the work, that person has responsibility for everything. In your databases, you will—by design—have many people able to access your data, but you may not want them to access everything in the same way. Roles are a way to divide up that work and limit what people can query, add, or modify. There are two parts to roles—the first is creating the role and the second is giving rights to the role.

They syntax to create a role uses the keywords—you got it— CREATE ROLE and then you give the name of the role. In our example we will create a role that only has access to dog information.

```
CREATE ROLE DogsOnly;

OUTPUT
Command(s) completed successfully.
```

We now have a role, but before it becomes useful to us we need to add permissions to the role. We will show that in the section below on Giving Access.

## SCHEMAS

As we mentioned earlier, a schema identifies the owner of an object and virtually all objects can have an owner. Most of the databases you will use will only have one schema; however, in some larger databases multiple schemas are often used.

Think of a schema as a way to group some of your objects together. This then allows you to give permissions to users or roles into that grouping rather than the individual objects.

# GIVING ACCESS

"The good Lord giveth, and the good Lord taketh away". While we have to be careful with the comparison, those are the two main ideas in database security—we can give access and we can take access away. On tables and views, we can give access in the following areas:

Table 4 Fundamental Permission Options

| Keyword | Permission |
|---------|------------|
| Select | Can view data |
| Insert | Can add new data |
| Update | Can modify data |
| Delete | Can remove data |

These levels allow us to provide some granularity to the permissions. For example you may want to have some reporting users that can view data, but you don't want the users to be able to make changes to the data. We give access with the keyword GRANT, and we can remove access with the keyword REVOKE.

If we use the role we created above, and we want to give view permissions to the DogsOnly role, we would execute the following statements.

```
GRANT SELECT ON PetOwner TO DogsOnly;
GRANT SELECT ON Dog TO DogsOnly;
```

```
OUTPUT
Command(s) completed successfully.
```

This role would now have access to only view or select the data from the *PetOwner* and *Dog* tables. We could grant the same access to a user; or we can also grant rights on the schema, and every object in that schema would then be viewable to the user.

A common way to secure data is to put sensitive data into a separate table and limit the users that have access to that table. For example, we could create a role that would allow a user to see the owner, cat, and dog tables but not allow them to see the *VeterinarianVistHistory* table if we thought this data was sensitive. A more common example is the salary of an employee. We may want many people to see the name, department, and ID of an employee; however, we don't want everyone to see salary information. Creating another table and making a join between the *Employee* and the *Salary* tables allows us to grant everyone access to the employee table, and only those needed few to the salary table.

## SUMMARY
It is a best practice to consider security when creating objects in your database, only giving access to what the user or role needs to complete their assignment.

# LESSON 16
# CHANGING
# OBJECTS

*This lesson deals with additions or new requirements our database might need after the original objects have been created.*

Change, as they say, is constant. While it would be nice if once we created our objects we didn't have to alter them again, the reality is just as our data changes, the objects that support that data will often change as well. While making a change to a view is straightforward, changing a table can be a bit more complicated.

## CHANGING A TABLE

Two common changes we make to tables are modifying the data type of a column or adding a column to a table. When we modify a column, we can only make a change that will support the data currently in the table. For example, if we had a text column that was currently 60 characters in size and the column included some text that was 50 characters long, we would be unable to make the size of the column 40 characters because we already have data larger than that. We could grow the column size to 100 if we needed to hold larger data because that will not interfere with the data already in the table.

There are two parts to altering a table. First we use the keyword ALTER TABLE and provide the table name. Then we use the keyword ALTER COLUMN and provide the table name to specify the change. If we needed to store longer names in our *PetOwner* table, we could expand the OwnerName column from 60 to 100.

```
ALTER TABLE PetOwner ALTER COLUMN OwnerName VARCHAR
(100);
```

```
OUTPUT
Command(s) completed successfully.
```

## ADDING A COLUMN

We can add a column to the table by using the keywords ALTER TABLE, followed by the name of the table, and then use the keyword ADD and specify the column name and the data type. If we do not specify the column is required, the default is NULL, meaning optional. Adding a column for a nickname to our Dog table would use the statement below.

```
ALTER TABLE Dog ADD PetNickName VARCHAR(50);
OUTPUT
Command(s) completed successfully.
```

In most RDBMS, the column will be added to the end of the table. Because of the difficulty in switching the order of the columns, the columns are left in their default order and new columns are added at the end.

Note—some changes to a table are not allowed while data is present in the table. For example, if we have a column of data type VARCHAR (100) and there is a row with 100 characters in that column, we would be unable to change the data type to VARCHAR(60). Other changes actually require us to create a new table, migrate the data over and rename the table.

## ADDING A FOREIGN KEY

After a two tables we want to relate are created, we can create the link or relationship between these tables. We normally link a primary key in one table to a column in the second table. In chapter 13, we created a new table called *Fish* and we want to link this the *PetOwner* table. Let's link these two tables. The foreign key will exist on the Fish table because the primary key, *OwnerIdentifier*, belongs to the *PetOwner* Table.

Adding a foreign key uses several keywords beginning with ALTER TABLE. We then specify the name of the table where the foreign key will be created. This is sometimes called the child table. We use the keywords ADD CONSTRAINT with the name of the foreign key and the column it will use. Lastly we use the key word REFERENCES to link to the PRIMARY KEY column of the other or 'parent' table. Our foreign key is now created.

```
ALTER TABLE Fish ADD CONSTRAINT RefPetOwner6
FOREIGN KEY (OwnerIdentifier)
REFERENCES PetOwner(OwnerIdentifier)
```

## REMOVING TABLES

Once a table is no longer needed, the keyword DROP TABLE with the name of the table will remove the table from the system. Be careful—dropping a table in a production environment is normally a BIG deal.

DROP TABLE [TableName]

## VIEWS

Making a change to a view uses the keyword ALTER; however, a view does not have individual pieces to change—it is all or nothing. We change or alter a view using the same syntax as the CREATE VIEW statement, changing the word CREATE to ALTER. Let's change the view v_SearchForGarfield view to use a LIKE instead of an equal operator.

```
ALTER VIEW v_SearchForGarfield
AS
(
Select *
FROM Cat
WHERE Cat.NameOfCat LIKE 'Gar%'
);

OUTPUT
Command(s) completed successfully.
```

## SUMMARY

Using the keyword ALTER, we can change our tables, view, columns, and data types. Even though it is a new object, foreign keys are created using the alter table command as well.

# LESSON 17
# DATA TYPES

*This lesson reviews the common ways we categorize data in our databases.*

There is an old saying—at least I think it is old--"garbage in, garbage out". The same can be true for our data. Data types help keep our information the way we expect, and we can then depend on the data when we want to start reporting on it or manipulating it.

## Size Matters

Another consideration we need to make with our data types is the size of the container. Going back to our example of a sub shop counter—the bins are different sizes because they hold items of different size. If we used only the largest to hold everything, our counter would be much longer than it needs to be and there would be an increased cost to have a counter that large. It works the same in our database—we don't want to reserve more space than is need if the expectation does not warrant it. This is not to say we should be so conservative our bins aren't large enough for the data that does come—just start small and build up. Table 5 shows some common data types along with their storage size. The storage size is for every row in the column. They look tiny, but I promise you it adds up fast.

Table 5 Common Data Types

| Data Type Name | Description | Storage Size |
|---|---|---|
| BIGINT | Can hold whole number values from negative 9,223,372,036,854,775,808 to 9,223,372,036,854,775,807 | 8 bytes |
| BIT | Sometimes referred to true/false. Only two values are allowed— either 0 or 1. | 1 byte |
| CHAR() | Can store up to 8,000 characters. Requires a length in the column description, e.g. CHAR(10) would allow up to 10 characters. If less than 10 are entered, the column will fill the rest of the row with spaces. If Carlos were used in a VARCHAR(10) the result would be 'Carlos '. | 1 byte per character |
| DATETIME | Includes the date and time to the millisecond. | 8 bytes |
| DECIMAL() | Requires two components—the total length of the number and the number of digits after the decimal. DECIMAL(9,2) would allow seven digits to the left of the decimal and two after. You could go up to 9999999.99 with this format. Length varies by database, but most can store a maximum of 32 digits. | Dependent on the number of characters allowed. Less than 9 will be stored in 5 bytes. |
| INT | A whole number from - 2,147,483,648 to 2,147,483,647. | 4 Bytes |

| NCHAR() | The N stands for unicode support—I am not sure why they didn't name it UCHAR, but they didn't ask me. Apparently The ISO synonyms for nchar are national char and national character. Unicode support is generally reserved when dealing with foreign languages—most notably the Asian languages. Maximum length of 4000 characters. | 2 bytes each character |
| --- | --- | --- |
| NVARCHAR() | This data type will also support Unicode character, but will have variable column lengths—this is what the VAR stands for. This can hold up to 8,000 bytes, although SQL Server now has a MAX option to hold much more. | 2 bytes per character |
| SMALLINT | Can store a range of whole numbers from -32,768 to 32,767 | 2 Bytes |
| VARCHAR() | String data types of either fixed length or variable length with a maximum of 8,000. | 1 byte per character |

## WHEN TO USE SPECIFIC DATA TYPES

Here are some examples of when you might choose to use a certain data type

**BigInt** - When you have been using Integer values and think you might go beyond the 2,147,483,647 limit. Don't use this one by default.

**Bit** - When there are only two choices, this is a good option. Yes/No, On/Off, True/False. These are all good candidates for BIT column data types. Just stay consistent with which value is true and which is false. Name your columns such that it make sense. For example, we used KeptIndoors to indicate 1 for Yes and 0 for No. Don't then use IsManager with 0 for Yes and 1 for No. That will get confusing quick.

**Char** – This is best used when exact lengths are expected. ZIP codes, 4 digit pin, or Standard Codes would be good examples.

**DateTime** – This is one is easy—when you want to record a date, of course! Order dates, audit columns, or last login time are all examples.

**Decimal** – This is the default if you need to capture fractions of numbers. Money or percentages would be good candidates.

**Int** – When you need whole numbers. Counts, order numbers, and quantities are normally good examples. This is usually my default for auto incrementing primary key values.

**SmallInt** - Lookup fields where you know the total number of records are less than 32,000.

**VarChar** - When rows are not uniform and foreign languages are not used. Free-form text boxes or variable length fields like street addresses are good examples.


## CHAR VS VARCHAR

The big difference between a character data type and a variable character data type is the automatic adjustment of the column lengths—variables (VARCHAR) can be different lengths. I will normally choose CHAR when the length of the column is less than eight characters or when I know every record will be the same length—like a state abbreviation code or system code. I will normally choose variable character data types everywhere else, so I don't have to worry about added 'white space' when I query the table. Sure, I can get rid of the white space, but I'd have to add the removal logic on each query.

## CHAR VS NCHAR

To use Unicode or not to use Unicode—that is the question; and I am sure the path on your SQL journey will lead you to a conversation about which to use. I admit that I myself have generally favored not using Unicode, or, in other words, using CHAR, unless I knew foreign languages were to be used. A recent Twitter interchange I had with some very smart folks has me rethinking this. The reality is more and more applications—especially those on the web—will eventually need to include foreign language support. Mergers, growth, or whatever fate has set will eventually drive the need to use Unicode, and while it does take up a bit more space, the small overhead is almost insignificant. Drive space is getting cheaper all the time and the need to support Unicode will only increase.

The other big drawback for Unicode formats is they only support up to 4,000 characters. Chances are you will have to implement some logic to deal with that, or use a larger data type—but these are generally specific to each RDBMS.

Now that is not to say non-Unicode formats are dead. They still have their place.

## Table 6 Some examples of using Unicode vs non-Unicode

| When to use Unicode | When it is ok not to worry about it. |
| --- | --- |
| Information entered by an end-user | Information entered by the system, or a standard. |
| First and Last Name | Codes assigned by internal policy, a 3$^{rd}$ party, or the law. |
| Address Information | Identifiers or abbreviations (IE A for Alpha, B for Bravo, etc.) |
| Comments or Text Areas | |

**SUMMARY**

The data types play a big role in your database and I am sure you will find yourself in arguments about data types soon. ☺ Try to be as specific as you can, but allow yourself some wiggle room for future changes.

# LESSON 18
# ADVANCED
# FEATURES

*This lesson deals with supporting objects that can help make your data safer and easier to report on.*

We have covered the basic syntax and concepts you will need to build queries. In this section, we will review some of the more advanced concepts. Not that they are overly difficult, they just require a little time and effort. They also represent an area often neglected by data professionals, which is unfortunate because they only serve to help protect the data and make it more accessible.

## CONSTRAINTS

We all have something that prevents us from doing something. Maybe you are too tired, too lazy, or don't have the money. Perhaps time has caught up with you and your options are now limited, or perhaps there is a law that prevents the activity you are pursuing. Each of these represent a constraint. We can apply the same logic in a database to prevent certain data from entering the database. While that may sound a bit backwards, believe it or not, a constraint can be your best friend when you are the person responsible for pulling data out of the system.

If we aren't careful about what data we put into the database, and how the data is put into the database, we may very well have a difficult time getting the correct data we want out of the system.

Your current responsibilities may not include creating database objects; however, you are probably interacting with data and will add additional data to the system. Understanding why constraints have been added to the database might help alleviate some of the frustration you feel when you run into them.

We have already looked at two types of constraints we have in the database. The data type of a column may not by definition be a constraint; however, if you have a column with a Date data type, good luck entering text into the field. The size of the data types are also another kind of constraint. If more characters are entered than the data type allows, an error will be generated. Sure, sometimes a table was created with little thought about how long the column would be and it ends up being short; however, you should also be asking—Is this length really what I am expecting? If so, we can enlarge the column length. If not, you can figure out how to change the data to make it work.

Another type of constraint we discussed earlier is the requirement condition of each column in the table. While the default is NULL, this still tells a user who wants to insert data what the minimum required fields are. If you want to see a row with no data, than you don't need to set this on your columns, but I believe you will find that a bit difficult to query against.

## Other types of constraints

### Unique
When each row must have a different value than any of the other values in the column, we use a UNIQUE constraint to help enforce this.

By default, our Primary Keys include this type of constraint. We can only have one value for each row in our table.

### Foreign Key
We talked in lesson 6 about how tables can be related for join purposes. A foreign key (FK) is a column or combination of columns that is used to establish and enforce a link between the data in two tables. You can create a foreign key by defining a FOREIGN KEY constraint when you create or modify a table.

A foreign key constraint will require the value exist in the first table before a value can be inserted into the second table. This is usually thought of as a hierarchy relationship with a parent table and a child table. It is also referred to as "one to many"—meaning, I can have one parent value and many children instances of that. In our example, a single pet could go to the vet many times. There will be only one record in a pet table for the pet, but there could be many rows in the veterinary record table for a pet. A foreign key constraint will require the pet record to be created first before the veterinary record can be created.

### Check
We can use a check constraint to ensure the value of the column is within some bound set by business rules. A

check constraint can be set on a table or a column. A column check constraint limits the values of the columns based on the criteria of the check. A check constraint on a table can make the values of one column conditional on the value of another column in the table.

## Default
When no value is specified when a record is created, a Default constraint can add a value to the record automatically. A very common default constraint is the current date on a column that keeps the date.

# INDEXES

As we query our database, we will become much more sensitive to the amount of data we want in our query results. Our examples are local to our computer and we are the only ones querying the database. As you get into bigger systems and have 10,000 people or 100,000 people querying the database you will begin to notice a performance decrease. This is where indexes come in. If we write smart queries with only the columns we need, and good WHERE clause statements, we can create a copy of the columns we need in the index. These indexes can increase our performance tremendously.

When we talk about indexes, there are two types.

## CLUSTERED INDEXES

Each table can have only one clustered index. The clustered index dictates the order the data is sorted and includes all the columns in the table. When we create a primary key, a clustered index is created using the primary key.

## NON-CLUSTERED INDEXES

Normally we create a clustered index first and then additional indexes in the database. These indexes are called non-clustered indexes and can include any number of columns. They create a second copy of the data. We don't have to include the primary key of the table in the non-clustered index as this automatically gets included in the index.

NO FREE LUNCH

While the use of indexes is absolutely required for good database performance, there is, as they say, no free lunch. Indexes create a second copy of the data. This causes the database to do a little extra work because all the inserts, updates, and deletes must now be performed in two places. While this is normally acceptable, best practices dictate we create only the indexes we need.

Indexes also require their own care and feeding. Normally the person who administers the database will perform this maintenance, but if that person is you, there is a bit of work to do. Check out some great maintenance scripts at http://ola.hallengren.com.

### Triggers

The great thing about computers is that we can tell it to do something and it will do it—unless you have a computer like mine. Just as we packaged some logic in a function, we can package some logic in the database that will get executed whenever the requested condition occurs. This is the good and the bad about triggers: they will get executed every time the condition is met. There are various ways we can implement triggers; however, the most common types of triggers are used when a record is created/inserted or when a record is updated/deleted.

A classic example of a trigger based on an update is an audit example. Suppose you wanted to keep all the history of a record, but only wanted to keep a single row in the table. You could create an update trigger that copied the 'old row,' or previous information, into an audit table when a row is updated.

While triggers can have their place, the best practice is to use the application to dictate most of the logic that can be done in a trigger. Troubleshooting a trigger can be tricky—especially when they are not properly documented.

As the logic we want to enforce is what dictates how a trigger is used, I have not included any SQL examples in the book.

## SUMMARY

Constraints help make your database better. Sure, they can be tough to work around sometimes, but when YOU are the query writer, you will be happy you have them. Indexes give the database specific information to help speed up your queries.

# LESSON 19
# LOOKING THE PART—FORMATTING AND BEST PRACTICES

*This lesson gives some thoughts on formatting and documentation*

When we talk about formatting and documentation there are as many opinions as there are ants in an ant farm. This admittedly can be more personal preference, but I will detail my reasons and I would be happy to hear other options.

## CAPITALIZATION

Ultimately, this lesson comes down to one point—readability. We want to provide a way for the person who has to look at this code, which could be you, to more easily understand it. To help in this cause, a little capitalization will do wonders. I suggest your keywords should be upper case, all your table and column names have the first letter of every word be capitalized, and everything else be in lower case. Examples of keywords are SELECT, UPDATE, DISTINCT, COUNT etc. All the examples in this book made use of this technique.

```
ALTER TABLE Dog ADD PetNickName VARCHAR(50)

SELECT DogIdentifier
FROM VeterinarianVisitHistory
WHERE RabiesShotCurrent = 0;
```

For sake of clarity, I spelled out all the words in the column name. Your database might be different. For example, a common shortening of the DogIdentifier would be DogId. The capitalization of each word lets the reader know there is more than one word that makes up the name. The database will treat DogID, Dogid, and DOGID all the same. This is all just for looks, which can cause plenty of heated arguments.

## WHITE SPACE

AreYouAbleToReadThisSentenceWithNoSpacing?     You probably can and the capitalization helps, but if the whole book was written that way you would have stopped reading a long time ago. White space is an important area in formatting and I have the following suggestions.

Do not include more than 3 columns on one line or a statement or query

FROM goes on a new line
`JOIN` should go on a new line
`WHERE` goes on a new line

Perhaps having all these columns on their own lines makes it long, but I won't go more than three on a line.

```
SELECT TOP 10  Cat.CatIdentifier, Cat.BirthDateOfCat,
Cat.BreedOfCat
       , Cat.ColorOfCat, Cat.KeptIndoors,
Cat.MonthsWithOwner
       , Cat.NameOfCat, Cat.OwnerIdentifier
       , Dog.DogIdentifier, Dog.BirthDateOfDog,
Dog.BreedOfDog
       , Dog.ColorOfDog, Dog.KeptIndoors,
Dog.MonthsWithOwner
       , Dog.NameOfDog
       , Dog.OwnerIdentifier

FROM Cat
INNER JOIN Dog ON Dog.OwnerIdentifier =
Cat.OwnerIdentifier;
```

## COMMENTS

Comments help the person viewing the code to know why you made some of the decisions you did. Writing a comment can be done in a couple of ways. In SQL Server Management Studio, comments are changed to a green color. Other RDBMS systems will have different behavior.

```
--Comments everything after the --, but just this line
```

I recommend against using the one line comment structure. There are scenarios where code can get mixed up with the line and you might comment out something that was supposed to run. The next person won't know and that code might be removed.

```
/*Will comment out

All lines until the closing is given.

*/
```

This is the preferred way to comment your code. When in doubt, leave a comment.

## THIRD PARTY TOOLS

If you are looking for some assistance with formatting, I suggest you check out the following:

SQL Server – ApexSQL has a free tool called SQL Refactor that allows you to choose different format options and will modify the code automagically.

Red Gate SQL Prompt – probably the most popular SQL assistant on the planet, SQL Prompt is much better than intellisence and has built in shortcuts to help you write your statements quickly.

## SUMMARY

While most of this can be debated, one idea is clear—be consistent in your writing and help your future self be able to read and understand the code. Don't be afraid to comment.

# LESSON 20: WORKING WITH DATES

*This lesson talks about how we can use dates in our queries.*

Many of the date examples will be RDBMS specific. The examples show here work in SQL Server with notes for Microsoft Access environments. If you would like to know more about your specific RDMBS, consider joining our Facebook page so you get personalized information for your specific needs.

## SYSTEM DATE AND TIME

Getting the system or current time is a very common task. Perhaps you want to know only records that have been added in the last 30 days. In order to complete that statement, you have to know what the current date and time are. The system can tell you it's time setting. Each time you run the query the correct date and time will be computed so if you run your query today, next week, or next month, you will only get the last 30 days of records.

```
SELECT GETDATE();
```

| RDBMS | Getting System Date |
|---|---|
| SQL Server | SELECT GETDATE() |
| Microsoft Access | SELECT DATE() |

## SPACE BETWEEN DATES

Another common question is the difference in time between two dates. For example, we have the birthdate of our animals, and like us they will get older every year. We want to write a query that will show us the age of our animals in years. To do this, we will use the DATEDIFF function. We will give the increment we want to measure, and then the beginning and ending dates, and the database will do the calculations. In this case, we want years.

```
SELECT Dog.NameOfDog,
DATEDIFF(YY,Dog.BirthDateOfDog,GETDATE())AS AgeOfDog
FROM DOG;

OUTPUT
(Modified)
NameOfDog         AgeOfDog
---------------   ----------
Odie              38
Laddie            7
Jack              3
Ace               5
Ace               11
(265 row(s) affected)
```

Table 7 below shows other interval options we can choose, and we can do calculations on those intervals. For example, in this case we will multiple by 7 to get the age of our cat in human years.

```
SELECT Cat.NameOfCat,
DATEDIFF(YY,Cat.BirthDateOfCat,GETDATE()),
DATEDIFF(YY,Cat.BirthDateOfCat,GETDATE()) * 7 AS
AgeInHumanYears
FROM Cat;
```

Output (Showing 5 rows)

| NameOfCat | AgeOfDog | AgeInHumanYears |
|-----------|----------|-----------------|
| Garfield | 37 | 259 |
| Ellie | 7 | 49 |
| Dexter | 3 | 21 |
| Arwen | 5 | 35 |
| Milo | 11 | 77 |

(273 row(s) affected)

Table 7 DateDiff Measurements

| DateDiff Abbreviation | Period of Time Measured |
|-----------------------|-------------------------|
| yyyy | Year |
| q | Quarter |
| m | Month |
| y | Day of year |
| d | Day |
| w | Weekday |
| ww | Week |
| h | Hour |
| n | Minute |
| s | Second |

## PARTS OF DATES

We may also want to extract only one part of a date from our column. For example, we might want to get a count of each year our dogs were born. In this example, we will use the YEAR function to extract only the year from the birth date column.

```
SELECT YEAR(Dog.BirthDateOfDog) AS BirthYear, COUNT(*)
'Number of Births'
FROM DOG
GROUP BY YEAR(Dog.BirthDateOfDog)
ORDER BY YEAR(Dog.BirthDateOfDog);
```

```
Output
BirthYear    Number of Births
----------   ----------------
1950         1
1978         1
2002         3
2003         24
2004         9
2005         8
2006         9
2007         8
2008         17
2009         36
2010         38
2011         7
2012         16
2013         20
2014         34
2015         34

(16 row(s) affected)
```

You might be asking yourself if there was a dog born in 1950 and 1978. Any thoughts on which dog that might be? We'll give the answer below the table.

Table 8 Common Date Functions

| Date Part | Function |
|-----------|----------|
| Year | YEAR() |
| Month Number | MONTH() |
| Day of the Month | MONTH() |

Snoopy from Peanuts first appeared in 1950 and Odie from Garfield first appeared in 1978.

**SUMMARY**

Working with dates will probably be the first advanced query writing you do. Using some of the built in functions, you can format and manipulate the dates to provide the data you want for a given time period.

# Congratulations!

You made it to the end. Welcome aboard the SQL trail, my new Compañero. I hope you enjoyed the book. If so, I would appreciate a positive review on Amazon. If you think something is missing, let me know at carlos.chacon@sqldatapartners.com. I look forward to hearing from you.

The website zerotosql.com will have additional information as I look to get feedback from the readers about what additional content they would like to review.

# APPENDIX 1
# INSTALLING TEST DATA

To help you along your journey of learning SQL, I have created a small database with some example data. I also have all of the scripts shown in the book available at http://zerotosql.com/zerotosqlscripts. I do ask for your email so you can become my compañero and join me on the SQL trail. I look forward to our journey together.

There are three scripts available in a zip folder; however, you will need to have SQL Server installed first. We will first create and populate a database. You can then open the second script with all the examples. The third script is some optional components you can run to enhance your experience.

## CREATING TEST DATABASE IN SQL SERVER

There are two options get up and running with SQL Server. As part of the download, a SQL Server 2012 database is included with the scripts. You can restore this database to your system and then begin the lessons; however, you should be familiar with restoring before you choose this option.

## To Restore via SQL Server Management Studio (SSMS)

1. In Object Explorer within SSMS and connect to a test instance of the SQL Server Database Engine.
2. Right-click the Databases folder and then click Restore Database.
3. To specify the source and location of the backup sets to restore, click the Device option under Source.
   - Click the browse button. In the Specify backup devices dialog box click Add.
   - Choose the ZeroToSQL.bak you downloaded from our site.
   - Click OK
4. Make sure the box is checked under the Backups sets to restore area and then click OK.

The database will be restored with the Name LearnSQL.

## To Restore with Scripts

To create the test database in SQL Server using scripts, you can follow these steps:

1. Once SQL Server has been installed, Create a new database through SQL Server Management Studio (SSMS) by connecting to a test database in object explorer and right clicking **New Database**.
   a. Enter the name **LearnSQL** in the database name text box.
   b. Click OK.
   c. The new database will be created

2. Open and execute (run) the file CreateObjects SQLServer.sql. This file contains the scripts needed to create all the example tables.

3. Open and execute the file InsertQueries SQLServer.sql. This file will insert all the sample records we will use.

There is another file, InsertOptionalValues.sql that can be used once you get to lesson 11, but it is not recommended you run InsertOptionalValues.sql until you get to that chapter.

To follow along with the examples in the book, open the file SQLServerQueries.sql and  the queries from the book are available for you to execute or modify as you see fit. If you do modify the scripts, the results you see in the book may not be  what you  see in your results window.

# APPENDIX 2
# RUNNING EXAMPLE IN THE REAL WORLD

This example we have been using during the book has one big drawback—I would not use it in the real world. In our example, we created a different table for cats and dogs. In the real world, I would have created a single pet table with a column that indicates what kind of animal they have and make the column names a bit more generic.

This is called normalization and you can read about it from your search engine of choice. Mine happened to pull up this as the first result. (https://en.wikipedia.org/wiki/Database_normalization)

I chose not to do this because the join diagrams of cats and dogs in lesson 6 are replicas of the drawing a co-worker drew for me when the lights finally clicked on join types. When I started writing this book, I knew I wanted to include these same diagrams and then I created a model around it. If this caused some confusion, I do apologize; however, you should know there is a better way to model the data we use in this book.

# INDEX

How can I make this index better?
Please let me know at carlos.chacon@sqldatapartners.com

How can I make this index better?
Please let me know at carlos.chacon@sqldatapartners.com

How can I make this index better?
Please let me know at carlos.chacon@sqldatapartners.com

How can I make this index better?
Please let me know at carlos.chacon@sqldatapartners.com

50834690R00074

Made in the USA
San Bernardino, CA
05 July 2017